Grade 5

W9-AXK-304

McGraw-Hill Reading

Wonders

Your Turn
Practice Book

Education

Bothell, WA • Chicago, IL • Columbus, OH • New York, NY

www.mheonline.com/readingwonders

The *McGraw-Hill* Companies

Mc Graw Hill **Education**

Copyright © The McGraw-Hill Companies, Inc.

Send all inquiries to:
McGraw-Hill Education
2 Penn Plaza
New York, NY 10121

Printed in the United States of America.

6 7 8 9 QVS 17 16 15 14

Contents

Unit 1 • Eureka! I've Got It!

Contents

Unit 2 • Taking the Next Step

Contents

Unit 3 • Getting from Here to There

Contents

Unit 4 • It's Up to You

Contents

Unit 5 • What's Next?

New Perspectives

Better Together

Our Changing Earth

Now We Know

TIME For Kids

Contents

Unit 6 • Linked In

Name _____

risk	afford	profit	savings
loan	wages	prosper	scarce

Use each pair of vocabulary words in a single sentence.

1. afford, loan

_____

_____

2. prosper, profit

_____

_____

3. savings, scarce

_____

_____

4. risk, wages

_____

_____

Name _____

Read the selection. Complete the sequence graphic organizer.

Characters

Setting

Beginning

Middle

End

Name _____

Read the passage. Use the reread strategy to make sure you understand what you have read.

Building Our Community

	"Hey, Mom," I said, dropping my backpack on the table. "Marla and I
13	were hoping you could take us to the mall next weekend."
24	"Sorry, Tasha, I'm working at the hospital this weekend and next
35	weekend," she said.
38	"Well, then what about Kevin?" I persisted, not ready to give up.
50	"Maybe he could take us."
55	Mom smiled at my determination, but her answer was firm. "First of all,
68	you and Marla need a parent chaperone with you at the mall to keep you
83	safe. Second, Kevin is volunteering next weekend by giving time to help
95	build a home for a family that needs one."
104	As soon as she said that, I remembered the way Kevin's eyes had lit
118	up when he'd first told us about the project. He's always been good at
132	building and fixing things. Now that he was seventeen, he was finally
144	old enough to take part in the home-building projects that our community
156	did twice a year.
160	"It's not fair," I complained. "Kevin can make a real difference
171	in a family's life, but what can I do? I'm not old enough to help
186	build the house."
189	Mom put on her serious face, which meant that she was about to give
203	advice. "Don't think about it like that, Tasha" she said. "People don't
215	make a difference by focusing on what they *can't* do. They change things
228	by thinking about what they *can* do."
235	I slunk off to my room as Mom's words echoed in my head over and
250	over. Maybe she was right. I might not be able to physically raise the roof
265	on the new house, but what I *could* raise was money to help.

Name _____

The next day, I talked to my teacher about raising money to help build the house. "Well, there's not much time to put something together," Mr. Pham said thoughtfully, "but, we can brainstorm about it this morning. It's our class's turn to sell water at the soccer game this weekend. I bet your classmates will have some good ideas about what else we could sell to raise money. Teamwork will be the best way to make this happen."

Building Our Community Sale
T-shirts $5

After roll call, Mr. Pham gave me the floor to explain my idea. Brason raised his hand. "My uncle owns a T-shirt shop. Maybe he can print some shirts that we can sell."

"Great idea!" Mr. Pham said enthusiastically. "Now, if Brason can get shirts for us, we need something to put on them. Any ideas?" After a lively debate, we settled on "Building Our Community" as our slogan. Marla, our class artist, agreed to draw the design.

The next day, Brason announced that his uncle would donate 20 shirts. Marla shared her sketch of interlocked hands. Now, we had to get the word out.

By Friday, we were ready. I had posted details about the sale on our class Web page and taped flyers in hallways and the cafeteria. The T-shirts, our merchandise, were printed.

Our Saturday sale was a success. We earned $125. Some people bought shirts. Others gave a dollar or two to our cause.

Kevin drove me to the local hardware store to buy a gift card that could be used for hammers, nails, lumber, and other equipment.

On the Friday before building was to start, our class took a field trip to the community center. I beamed with pride as I handed over the gift card. Mom and Mr. Pham had both been right. Everyone can do something, and together we can accomplish something great.

Name _____

A. Reread the passage and answer the questions.

1. **Underline the words in each sentence that are clues to sequence.**

    The next day, Brason announced that his uncle would donate 20 shirts.

    By Friday, we were ready.

2. **Write the sentence from the story that tells when Tasha told the class about her idea. Underline the words that are a clue to sequence.**

    _____

    _____

3. **What four things happened between the time Marla agreed to draw a design for the T-shirts and the day of the sale?**

    _____

    _____

    _____

    _____

B. Work with a partner. Read the passage aloud. Pay attention to expression and accuracy. Stop after one minute. Fill out the chart.

	Words Read	–	Number of Errors	=	Words Correct Score
First Read		–		=	
Second Read		–		=	

Name _____

A Neighborhood Need

"Did you hear that Mr. Green's Corner market closed?" Jayla asked Casey.

"Yeah," Casey replied. "Now my mom has to go all the way across town to buy fruits and vegetables."

"In the library, I saw a sign about a farmer's co-op. If they have enough customers, they will bring fresh fruits and vegetables to us," said Jayla.

"Then let's figure out a way to get neighbors signed up," said Casey.

"We can't get fresh vegetables here."

Answer the questions about the text.

1. **How do you know this text is realistic fiction?**

   _____

   _____

2. **Do you think the dialogue in this text is a good example of what people might say in real life? Why or why not?**

   _____

   _____

3. **What details does the illustration show you that you did not find in the text?**

   _____

   _____

4. **List two things about the setting in the illustration that are realistic.**

   _____

   _____

Name _____

Read each passage. Underline the context clues that help you figure out the meaning of each word in bold. Then write the word's meaning on the line.

1. "Marla and I were hoping you could take us to the mall next weekend." "Sorry, Tasha, I'm working at the hospital this weekend and next weekend," she said. "Well, then what about Kevin?" I **persisted**, not ready to give up. "Maybe he could take us."

   _____

2. Kevin is **volunteering** next weekend by giving time to help build a home for a family that needs one.

   _____

3. I slunk off to my room as Mom's words **echoed** in my head over and over. Maybe she was right.

   _____

4. "Now, if Brason can get shirts for us, we need something to put on them. Any ideas?" After a lively **debate**, we settled on "Building Our Community" as our slogan. Marla, our class artist, agreed to draw the design.

   _____

5. "Now, if Brason can get shirts for us, we need something to put on them. Any ideas?" After a lively debate, we settled on "Building Our Community" as our **slogan**. Marla, our class artist, agreed to draw the design.

   _____

Name _____

A. Read the words in the box. Place each word in the column that describes its short vowel sound. Underline the letter or letters that make the sound.

bread	nick	scan	rough	blond
shrug	ship	tense	damp	cot
click	notch	laugh	gush	tenth

short *a*	short *e*	short *i*	short *o*	short *u*

B. Circle the word with the short vowel sound to complete the sentence.

1. My brother is the _____ chef that I have ever met.

   worst   best   only

2. Do you enjoy going to _____ each year?

   school   work   camp

3. Please _____ the door before you leave for the day.

   close   lock   seal

4. The _____ rose up over the mountains.

   mist   cloud   storm

Name _____

> *Evidence* is details and examples from a text that support a writer's ideas. The student who wrote the paragraph below cited evidence that shows how illustrations give important details about characters and events.
>
> **Topic sentence** → The illustration in "Building Our Community" gives important details about an event that is not described in the story. The illustration shows what happened during the fundraiser Tasha and her classmates put together. The illustration shows that the class put up an ad for the sale. It shows that the T-shirts cost $5. It also shows that the characters worked together and were happy. All these details in the illustration give important information that is not described in the story.
>
> **Evidence** →
>
> **Concluding statement** →

Write a paragraph about the text you have chosen. Cite evidence to show how an illustration gives important details about characters or events. Remember to clearly state the topic and to write in complete sentences.

Write a topic sentence: _____

_____

Cite evidence from the text: _____

_____

_____

_____

_____

_____

_____

End with a concluding statement: _____

_____

Name _____

A. Read the draft model. Use the questions that follow the draft to help you think about what descriptive details you can add.

Draft Model

Kim walked to class. Something was wrong. She thought she might flunk math. I helped her. Pretty soon she was doing much better.

---

1. How might Kim's walk and expression show that she is unhappy?

2. Is something badly wrong or just a little upsetting? What details would help the reader understand this?

3. What details would show how the narrator helps Kim?

4. What is a more descriptive way to tell how Kim was feeling by the end?

B. Now revise the draft by adding details that help readers learn more about Kim and how she felt.

_____

_____

_____

_____

_____

_____

_____

_____

_____

_____

_____

Name _____

anxious	assemble	decipher	distracted
navigate	retrace	accomplish	options

Write a complete sentence to answer each question below. In your answer, use the vocabulary word in bold.

1. Why might a student **assemble** books and magazines that are all on the same subject?

   _____

   _____

2. Why might campers lost in the woods **retrace** their steps?

   _____

3. How could you **decipher** a passage written in another language?

   _____

4. What **options** do students have to improve their work in school?

   _____

   _____

5. Why is a **distracted** driver a dangerous driver?

   _____

   _____

6. What is a way to **accomplish** a task more quickly?

   _____

7. What can you use to help you **navigate** from one place to another?

   _____

8. Why do some people feel **anxious** in a thunderstorm?

   _____

Name _____

Read the selection. Complete the problem and solution graphic organizer.

Character

Setting

Problem

Events

Solution

Name _____

Read the passage. Use the reread strategy to check your understanding of the story.

A Race Against the Clock

13	Lian gazed in awe at the giant redwood trees towering far overhead. Her
25	family's vacation to Northern California had been full of fun activities and
38	historic sites. Getting to see the majestic redwoods was icing on the cake.
49	Lian's father interrupted her thoughts. "Shake a leg everyone," he said,
60	clapping his hands quickly. "We don't want to miss our flight."
72	Lian and her older brother Shing hurried back to the family's rental
84	car. Their mother was already in the front passenger seat, drumming her
95	fingertips against the center console. Lian knew her mother was worried
109	about missing their flight home. Mrs. Yee had wanted to stay close to the
121	airport during the last morning of their vacation, but everyone else wanted
131	to see the giant redwood trees. She finally gave in.
145	Mr. Yee slid into the driver's seat. "We have two hours before we need
159	to check in at the airport," he said, checking his watch. "We'll have plenty
163	of time to spare."
175	Lian admired the trees as they drove through the park. Shing's attention,
187	however, was focused elsewhere. "Hey, Dad, I think you were supposed to
199	turn there," he said, pointing over his shoulder at a road marker.
211	"Good catch, Shing," replied Mr. Yee. It took several minutes to find
225	a place to turn around on the narrow road. They retraced their route and
237	tried again. This time, Lian and Shing kept their eyes peeled watching
	for markers.

Name _____

Lian and Shing spent the next hour chatting quietly in the backseat. Their conversation was interrupted by a loud "Bang!" as Lian's side of the car abruptly sagged low to the ground.

Mr. Yee calmly slowed down and pulled the car to the side of the road. "Everybody stay in the car," he ordered. He turned on the hazard lights and got out to inspect the car. Mrs. Yee was on the phone with the rental company when he returned. "The axle is damaged," he sighed.

After a few moments of discussion, it was decided that the rental company would send a taxi to take the family to the airport, and a tow truck would haul the car to a repair shop. Lian was on pins and needles while they waited. What would happen if they missed their flight? She was still nervous when the taxi arrived. They swiftly piled into the yellow van, her father riding shotgun next to the taxi driver.

The driver was upbeat. "I'll have you folks at the airport in two shakes of a lamb's tail," he said. "Traffic shouldn't be a problem at this time of day."

Unfortunately, traffic was a problem. A line of slow-moving cars snaked around the airport. The taxi came to a halt three blocks away from the main terminal. Mr. Yee groaned.

Mrs. Yee made a decision. "Kids, grab your things. If we hurry, we can still catch our flight," she said. Mr. Yee paid the driver while Mrs. Yee, Lian, and Shing retrieved their luggage from the trunk. Suitcases in hand, they jogged past the line of stopped cars.

The Yees hurried through the airport and made it to their gate with just minutes to spare. As they caught their breath before boarding the plane, Mrs. Yee looked at her family and grinned. "Next time, we stay near the airport," she said.

The Yee family raced toward the airport.

Name _____

A. Reread the passage and answer the questions.

1. What is the main, or most important problem in the text?

_____

_____

2. What are two important problems the Yees encounter on their way to the airport?

_____

_____

_____

3. How are each of these problems solved in the text?

_____

_____

_____

B. Work with a partner. Read the passage aloud. Pay attention to intonation. Stop after one minute. Fill out the chart.

	Words Read	–	Number of Errors	=	Words Correct Score
First Read		–		=	
Second Read		–		=	

Name _____

Building a Team

Noah's class, as a group, was assigned to navigate the obstacle course. He was first in line and anxiously wondered, "How can I help my team?"

The first task was to walk the length of a swinging log, a foot off the ground. Noah found it was easy for him to balance and reach the other side. Then he had a realization. He could help "spot," or guide, classmates who were less athletic than he. *That*, he decided, would be his contribution to his team!

Answer the questions about the text.

1. **How do you know this text is realistic fiction?**

   _____

   _____

2. **What gave Noah confidence and an idea of how to contribute to his team?**

   _____

   _____

3. **What words in the first paragraph show suspense?**

   _____

   _____

4. **Why do these words create a feeling of suspense?**

   _____

   _____

Name _____

Read each passage below. Underline the words that give a clue to the meaning of each idiom in bold. Then explain the idiom on the lines.

1. Lian's father interrupted her thoughts. **"Shake a leg** everyone," he said, clapping his hands quickly. "We don't want to miss our flight."

   _____

   _____

2. The driver was upbeat. "I'll have you folks at the airport **in two shakes of a lamb's tail**," he said. "Traffic shouldn't be a problem at this time of day."

   _____

   _____

3. After a few moments of discussion, it was decided that the rental company would send a taxi to take the family to the airport, and a tow truck would haul the car to a repair shop. Lian was **on pins and needles** while they waited. What would happen if they missed their flight? She was still nervous when the taxi arrived.

   _____

   _____

4. They swiftly piled into the yellow van, her father **riding shotgun** next to the taxi driver.

   _____

   _____

Name _____

Write three words from the box that have the same long vowel sound as the example in each row. Then underline the letter or letters that make the long vowel sound.

greed	music	spice	paste	unit
oak	plead	fuse	bride	growth
shave	folks	theme	paid	grind

1. rake _____ _____ _____

2. feet _____ _____ _____

3. kite _____ _____ _____

4. flow _____ _____ _____

5. cute _____ _____ _____

Name _____

Evidence is details and examples from a text that support a writer's opinion. The student who wrote the paragraph below cited evidence that supports his or her opinion about how well two authors create a feeling of suspense.

Topic sentence ⟶   I think "A Race Against the Clock" is a more suspenseful story than "Whitewater Adventure." In "A Race Against the Clock," the author includes details and dialogue that show

Evidence ⟶ that Mr. and Mrs. Yee are worried that they will miss their flight. The Yee family also faces many problems that slow them down along the way to the airport. In "Whitewater Adventure," Nina's parents do not show that they are worried and the family is able to solve their problem quickly. The

Concluding statement ⟶ details the author used in "A Race Against the Clock" create more suspense than the details in "Whitewater Adventure."

Write a paragraph about two texts you have chosen. Cite evidence from the texts to support your opinion about how well the authors create a feeling of suspense. Remember to include a strong closing and to include sentences that use subjects and predicates correctly.

Write a topic sentence: _____

_____

Cite evidence from the texts: _____

_____

_____

_____

_____

_____

End with a concluding statement: _____

_____

Name _____

A. Read the draft model. Use the questions that follow the draft to help you think about how it could be revised to improve its style and tone.

Draft Model

Macy saw her favorite baseball player. He was big. He talked to her. She got his autograph.

---

1. How could sentence structure and word choice be changed to create an engaging style and positive tone?

2. What descriptive details could be added to help the reader visualize the action?

3. What details could be added to convey Macy's enthusiasm?

4. What details could be added to describe the people and the actions in this draft?

B. Now revise the draft by adding details to create an engaging style and to convey Macy's positive feelings about getting the autograph.

_____

_____

_____

_____

_____

_____

_____

_____

_____

_____

Name _____

| debris | emphasis | encounter | generations |
| indicated | naturalist | sheer | spectacular |

Finish each sentence using the vocabulary word provided.

1. **(debris)** The storm last night _____

_____.

2. **(emphasis)** The park ranger repeated _____

_____.

3. **(encounter)** While walking in the woods, _____

_____.

4. **(generations)** Our family _____

_____.

5. **(indicated)** The frost on the leaves _____

_____.

6. **(naturalist)** We brought the strange plant _____

_____.

7. **(sheer)** Our guide led us away _____

_____.

8. **(spectacular)** The Fourth of July fireworks _____

_____.

Name _____

Read the selection. Complete the cause and effect graphic organizer.

Cause	➡	Effect
	➡	
	➡	
	➡	
	➡	

Name _____

Read the passage. Use the ask and answer questions strategy to help you understand new facts or difficult explanations.

At Home in the Desert

	Georgia O'Keeffe always thought of herself as an artist. By 1928, the
12	rest of the world did, too. At the age of 41 she was living in New York
29	City and becoming a well-known painter. She was married to a famous
41	photographer, who helped her show her work. Still, O'Keeffe wasn't
51	happy.
52	New York City and her family's summer home had been the source of
65	ideas for almost ten years. Now those ideas were drying up. O'Keeffe felt
78	like she needed a change of scenery. She had visited New Mexico in 1917
92	with her sister. The wide open space had thrilled her. "Maybe I should go
106	back," she thought to herself.
111	Her friend Mabel Dodge Luhan encouraged her. In April of 1929,
122	O'Keeffe packed her bags. She went to stay with Luhan in her home in
136	Taos, New Mexico. O'Keeffe wrote to her husband,
144	"Mabel's place beats anything you can imagine
151	about it—it is simply astonishing."
157	The wide open space drew O'Keeffe in. She spent hours just watching
169	the sky change. The clear light made her feel as if she could see for the
185	first time.
187	The beauty of the land renewed her. She couldn't wait to start painting.
200	Cow and horse skulls and desert flowers filled her canvases. The colors
212	of the desert inspired O'Keeffe to make new choices in her artwork. "The
225	color up there is different," she explained. She loved the blue-greens in the
238	sagebrush along the mountainsides.

Name _____

That August, O'Keeffe went home to New York. It was the start of a pattern she would keep up for almost twenty years. Each spring, she traveled to New Mexico to paint. These trips were vital to her spirit. Then, in the fall, she would return to New York to show her work.

During each visit to New Mexico, O'Keeffe explored her surroundings more deeply. Every day was an adventure. In the morning, she would set out to search for new desert scenes to paint. She kept a canvas and brushes in the backseat of her car. Whenever something caught her eye, she could pull them out and begin painting.

The desert landscape enchanted Georgia O'Keeffe.

The bleached animal bones and skulls that O'Keeffe found especially excited her. She saw a strange beauty in them. By experimenting, she found new ways to represent them in her paintings. The bones didn't symbolize death to O'Keeffe. To her, they showed the lasting beauty of the desert.

The unique landscapes, clear light, and bright colors spoke to her. She often painted close-ups of the rocks and mountains. Later, she began to travel more in search of new ideas. However, she always came back to New Mexico. After all these years, it was her home.

As O'Keeffe grew older, her eyesight began to fail. Continuing to paint became difficult. Still, O'Keeffe wasn't ready to stop working. Her friend Juan Hamilton helped her work with watercolors. He also taught her to sculpt with clay. With his aid, she made art into her 90s. When she died at the age of 98, Hamilton sprinkled her ashes over the desert. Her body became part of the land that had touched her art and her life.

Name _____

A. Reread the passage and answer the questions.

1. What caused Georgia O'Keeffe to seek out a change in her life?

_____

_____

_____

2. What evidence in the fifth paragraph shows the effect of O'Keeffe's visit to New Mexico?

_____

_____

_____

3. How did Georgia O'Keeffe react to her failing eyesight in her later years?

_____

_____

_____

B. Work with a partner. Read the passage aloud. Pay attention to expression and phrasing. Stop after one minute. Fill out the chart.

	Words Read	−	Number of Errors	=	Words Correct Score
First Read		−		=	
Second Read		−		=	

Name _____

A New Agency

During the 1960s, people grew concerned about the environment. This concern led to a huge Earth Day celebration in April of 1970. Politicians promised to find ways to improve water, land, and air quality. President Richard Nixon agreed to meet this new challenge. He proposed creating a new government department in late 1970. It was called the Environmental Protection Agency. Nixon said he hoped the EPA would "ensure the protection, development and enhancement of the total environment."

The EPA proposed laws that reduced air pollution from car engines.

Answer the questions about the text.

1. How can you tell that this text is narrative nonfiction?

_____

_____

2. Explain the cause and effect relationship between Earth Day and the creation of the EPA.

_____

_____

3. What facts about President Richard Nixon does the text give?

_____

_____

4. What primary source can you identify in this text?

_____

Name _____

Read each passage below. Underline the context clues that help you figure out the meaning of each word in bold. Write the word's meaning on the line. Then write your own sentence that uses the word in the same way.

1. Georgia O'Keeffe thought of herself as an artist. By 1928, the **rest** of the world did, too.

   _____

   _____

2. New York City and her family's summer home had been the source of ideas for almost ten years. Now those ideas were drying up. O'Keeffe felt like she needed a **change** of scenery.

   _____

   _____

3. She had visited New Mexico in 1917 with her sister. The wide open **space** had thrilled her.

   _____

   _____

4. She spent hours just watching the sky change. The clear **light** made her feel as if she could see for the first time.

   _____

   _____

5. It was the start of a pattern she would keep up for almost twenty years. Each **spring**, she traveled to New Mexico to paint.

   _____

   _____

Name _____

A. Read the words below. Place each word in the column that describes its vowel sound. Underline the letters that stand for the vowel sound.

tuna	crooks	could	lose	mute
amuse	would	soothe	union	bruise
hoof	view	plume	hue	hooks

/ū/ as in *music*	/ù/ as in *hook*	/ü/ as in *scoop*
_____	_____	_____
_____	_____	_____
_____	_____	_____
_____	_____	_____

B. Circle the word with the /ū/, /ù/, or /ü/ sound to complete the sentence.

1. The car has enough _____ to last another hour.

   gas   power   fuel

2. There are _____ lanes open at the bowling alley.

   few   many   several

3. This summer I will read a _____.

   biography   cookbook   mystery

4. He tried to _____ that he was correct.

   prove   show   explain

Name _____

Evidence is details and examples from a text that support a writer's ideas. The student who wrote the paragraph below cited evidence that shows how the author uses Georgia O'Keeffe's own words to support an idea.

Topic sentence → In "At Home in the Desert," the author uses Georgia O'Keeffe's own words to show that New Mexico was important to the artist. The author includes the words

Evidence → that Georgia O'Keeffe wrote to her husband when she visited New Mexico. O'Keeffe wrote that the place was "astonishing." She went back to New Mexico for many visits. She said that "the color up there is different." She found new ways to paint because of what she saw there. The

Concluding statement → author's use of O'Keeffe's words supports the idea that New Mexico was important to her art and her life.

Write a paragraph about the text you have chosen. Cite evidence from the text that shows how the author uses another person's words to support an idea. Remember to give examples and to avoid run-on sentences.

Write a topic sentence: _____

_____

Cite evidence from the text: _____

_____

_____

_____

_____

_____

End with a concluding statement: _____

_____

Name _____

A. Read the draft model. Use the questions that follow the draft to help you think about what strong words you can add.

Draft Model

As I was working outside, I found a bird's nest in our tree. It had baby birds in it. I could hear them. The mother bird came back and fed the babies.

1. What vivid sensory details could describe the trees, nest, and birds?

2. What strong words and phrases could be substituted for "working outside," "found," and "came back"?

3. What words and phrases would show, rather than tell, what happened? What details would help the reader picture what is being described?

B. Now revise the draft by adding strong words that will help readers better visualize the encounter with the birds.

_____

_____

_____

_____

_____

_____

_____

_____

_____

_____

_____

_____

Name _____

enthusiastically   patents   devices   captivated

passionate   claimed   breakthrough   envisioned

Write a complete sentence to answer each question below. In your answer, use the vocabulary word in bold.

1. What is an activity that you do **enthusiastically?**

_____

2. Why should inventors get **patents** for their inventions?

_____

3. What are the two most helpful **devices** you use every day?

_____

4. Name something that recently **captivated** your imagination.

_____

5. How would you know if a person is **passionate** about baseball?

_____

6. If items in the lost and found at school are not **claimed,** what should happen to them?

_____

7. What is a **breakthrough** you have made when trying to learn something new?

_____

8. What is one type of technology you have **envisioned** for the future?

_____

Name _____

Read the selection. Complete the sequence graphic organizer.

Event

↓

↓

↓

Name _____

Read the passage. Use the ask and answer questions strategy to help you understand new facts or difficult explanations.

Mary Anderson and the First Windshield Wipers

The Problem

2	When some people see a problem, they jump in to solve it. Mary
15	Anderson was that type of person.
21	In the early 1900s, few people owned cars. Instead, they rode electric
33	streetcars, or trolleys. On a snowy day in New York City, Anderson
45	watched streetcar drivers struggle to see through their wet windshields.
55	At the time, drivers had two ways to clean their windshields. They
67	could open the windshield's middle window, or they could get out of the
80	streetcar. If drivers opened the window, the driver and riders got wet. If
93	drivers got out of the streetcar, they put themselves in danger.
104	Some people wiped their windows with a piece of onion or carrot. This
117	supposedly left behind an oily film that kept water off. Instead, it often
130	clouded the windshield.

The Solution

133	
135	Anderson sympathized with the streetcar drivers. She asked others
144	about the problem. Surely someone had tried to solve it. People told
156	Anderson the problem had been studied. No one had found an answer.
168	They did not think there was one.
175	Anderson did not accept this. She vowed to find a better way. Her
188	efforts led to a new technology.
194	She drew a diagram of a tool for cleaning windshields. Anderson
205	found someone to make a model for her. It was the first working model
219	of a "windshield wiper."

Name _____

The model had a lever that moved a swinging metal arm (D). The arm held a rubber blade (C). From inside the streetcar, the driver would turn a handle (E) connected to the lever. As the lever moved (B), the blade would "sweep across and clean the window-pane." The driver and riders stayed safe and dry. In good weather, the wipers could be removed.

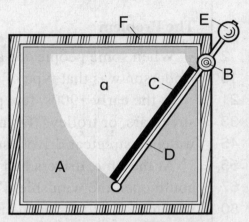

Mary Anderson's windshield cleaning device, as shown in her patent application.

Anderson applied for a patent for her "window cleaning device for electric cars . . . to remove snow, ice, or sleet from the window." A patent allows an inventor to sell his or her invention. Anderson wrote that she hoped to help streetcar drivers with "not being able to see through the front glass in stormy weather." In 1903 her patent was approved.

The Results

In 1905 Anderson tried to sell her device to a Canadian firm. Although the wipers worked, automobiles were still not very common. The company would not be able to sell many wipers. They would not make enough money. The firm turned her down. Anderson did not try to sell her wipers to anyone else.

Four years later, the first really popular car—Henry Ford's Model T—was released. Almost anyone could afford to buy a Model T. People who drove cars such as the Model T faced the same problem as streetcar drivers. How would they clean their windshields?

By 1913 thousands of cars had a version of Anderson's windshield wipers. Sadly, Anderson never made any money from her patent. Her breakthrough led to the next great idea, though. In 1917 another woman, Charlotte Bridgewood, invented automatic windshield wipers.

Name _____

A. Reread the passage and answer the questions.

1. **What time signal in the second paragraph helps you understand why cleaning windshields was such a problem?**

_____

_____

_____

2. **What four steps did Mary Anderson take after she noticed the problem streetcar drivers had cleaning their windshields?**

_____

_____

_____

_____

3. **What sequence of events explains why Anderson did not make any money from her patent?**

_____

_____

_____

_____

_____

B. Work with a partner. Read the passage aloud. Pay attention to expression and phrasing. Stop after one minute. Fill out the chart.

	Words Read	–	Number of Errors	=	Words Correct Score
First Read		–		=	
Second Read		–		=	

Name _____

Robot Creator

Tomotaka Takahashi lives and works in Japan. As a boy, he enjoyed reading comic books about robots, and he liked to build interesting devices. Now he builds robots that he hopes people will use in everyday life. Tomotaka does not want his robots to look like machines. He envisions them as friendly devices that look like people. He gives his robots extra movements to help them walk and move smoothly. People are captivated by Tomotaka's amazing robots.

Tomotaka's friendly looking robots walk and move like humans.

Answer the questions about the text.

1. **How do you know that this is biographical text?**

   _____

   _____

2. **Identify three facts about Tomotaka Takahashi that are included in the text.**

   _____

   _____

3. **What words and phrases introduce information about different times in Tomotaka's life?**

   _____

   _____

4. **How does the illustration help you understand more about the robots that Tomotaka creates?**

   _____

   _____

Name _____

Greek root	Meaning	Examples
ēlektron	amber	**elec**tric, **elec**tricity
pathos	feelings	sym**pathy**, em**pathy**
technē	art or skill	**techn**ology, **techn**ical
graph/gram	to write	photo**graph**, tele**gram**

Read each passage below. Use the Greek roots in the box above and sentence clues to help you figure out the meaning of the word in bold. Write the word's meaning on the line. Then write your own sentence that uses the word in the same way.

1. In the early 1900s, few people owned cars. Instead, they rode **electric** streetcars, or trolleys.

_____

_____

2. Anderson **sympathized** with the streetcar drivers. She asked others about the problem.

_____

_____

3. She vowed to find a better way. Her efforts led to a new **technology**.

_____

_____

4. She drew a **diagram** of a tool for cleaning windshields.

_____

_____

Name _____

A. Read each word in the box and listen for an *r*-controlled vowel sound. Write the word in the correct column below.

heart	scorn	before	spark
square	wear	harsh	coarse
chart	source	scarce	flare

/är/ as in *car*   **/âr/ as in *air***   **/ôr/ as in *born***

_____   _____   _____

_____   _____   _____

_____   _____   _____

_____   _____   _____

B. Read each sentence. Circle the words that have one of the *r*-controlled vowel sounds studied above.

1. She has a rare gemstone in her collection.

2. He will board the train at noon on Friday.

3. It is not polite to stare at other people.

4. They saw a deer in the glare of the headlights.

5. Please pour everyone some grape juice.

Name _____

Evidence is details and examples from a text that support a writer's ideas. The student who wrote the paragraph below cited evidence that compares how two authors present information about the same topic in different ways.

Topic sentence →   The author of "Mary Anderson and the First Windshield Wipers" and the author of "Fantasy Becomes Fact" give information about inventors in different ways. The author

Evidence →   of "Fantasy Becomes Fact" describes Arthur C. Clarke's inventions by describing events in his life from the age of 13 to adulthood. The author of "Mary Anderson and the First Windshield Wipers" tells about Mary's invention by focusing

Concluding statement →   on a problem Mary helped solve. Both ways of presenting information explain an inventor's accomplishments.

Write a paragraph about two texts that discuss similar topics. Cite evidence from the texts to compare how the authors present information in different ways. Remember to clearly state the topic and use conjunctions and commas correctly in complex sentences.

Write a topic sentence: _____

_____

Cite evidence from the texts: _____

_____

_____

_____

End with a concluding statement: _____

_____

Name _____

A. Read the draft model. Use the questions that follow the draft to help you think about how you can use time-order signal words to show the sequence of events.

<table>
<tr><td colspan="1">

Draft Model

Chen began preparing for the race. He ate a good breakfast. He did his stretching exercises. He got dressed. He left the house, determined to win.
</td></tr>
</table>

1. What time-order signal words could be added to show what Chen did first?

2. What other signal words could be added to make the sequence of events clearer?

3. What word or words could be added to the final sentence to give the text a sense of closure?

B. Now revise the draft by adding time-order signal words to help readers better understand the sequence of events.

_____

_____

_____

_____

_____

_____

_____

_____

_____

_____

_____

_____

_____

Name _____

| access | advance | analysis | cite |
| counterpoint | data | drawbacks | reasoning |

Use each pair of vocabulary words in a single sentence.

1. access, data

_____

_____

2. advance, reasoning

_____

_____

3. drawbacks, counterpoint

_____

_____

4. cite, analysis

_____

_____

Name _____

Read the selection. Complete the author's point of view graphic organizer.

Details		Author's Point of View
	→	

Name _____

Read the two passages by two different authors. Use the reread strategy to check your understanding of each author's position on this issue.

DO GENETICALLY MODIFIED FOODS BENEFIT THE WORLD?

The GMF Solution

3	*Genetically modified foods help fight malnutrition.*
9	Science has often provided answers to our problems. The development
19	of medicines, for example, helps cure diseases. Genetically modified
28	foods can be just as helpful. Genetically modified foods are foods whose
40	genes have been changed. A gene is a part of a cell that controls how a
56	living thing looks and functions. Farmers have changed genes in crops for
68	centuries by transferring pollen from one type of plant to another.

Science Lends a Hand

79	
83	Today, scientists can make the same types of changes much faster than
95	farmers can. Even though the scientists work in laboratories, their work is
107	not very different from what farmers were already doing.
116	Scientists can change crops in a more exact way. They have made
128	new types of corn that resist plant diseases and insects. These changes
140	mean farmers can use fewer chemicals on their crops. That means fewer
152	chemicals in our food and water, which helps protect the environment.

Better Food and More of It

163	
169	Scientists have also increased the nutrition in certain crops. They added
180	iron to rice and made other rice that helps bodies produce vitamin A. Such
194	genetically modified foods can fight malnutrition.
200	Genetically changed food can help fight world hunger in other ways,
211	too. Scientists can create crops that will grow in harsh conditions. They
223	can speed up and increase the harvest of crops. This will allow more food
237	to be grown and more people to be fed.
246	Genetically modified food may seem strange, but eventually people will
256	see that it holds the answers to many of the world's problems.

Name _____

A Risky Business

Genetically modified foods may not be safe.

Genetically modified foods might seem like science fiction, but they are already part of our everyday lives. Most processed foods in the United States, such as breakfast cereal, contain ingredients that have been genetically changed. Are those foods safe? We don't know.

Scientists Follow an Uncertain Path

When scientists genetically change food crops, they take genes from one species, or type of living thing—such as bacteria, and add those genes to the food crop. Scientists have not studied the long-term results of these interspecies changes or their effects on human health. For example, if a gene from fish was put into peas, would someone allergic to fish also be allergic to those peas? Scientists say no, but they have not tested the theory to be sure.

Some genes that have been added to crops are unaffected by antibiotics. Antibiotics are medicines that fight diseases caused by bacteria. What happens when people eat food that has these genes? Will they become less able to fight off illness? We do not know.

Future Effects on the Environment

What about the environmental effects of genetically modified food? Farmers have seen pollen carried from genetically modified corn to natural corn. Could this change natural corn? Could genetically modified crops that are resistant to insects cause some insects to die off, creating an imbalance in the ecosystem?

All this uncertainty should lead us to develop genetically modified foods with extreme caution, if at all.

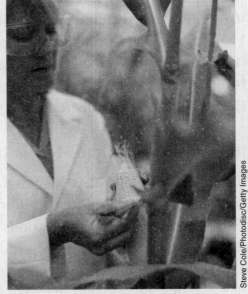

Genetically modifying food crops may produce both benefits and problems.

Name _____

A. Reread the passage and answer the questions.

1. What is an example the first author gives of how science has solved a problem?

    _____

    _____

2. What are two ways the first author thinks genetically modified foods are better?

    _____

    _____

3. What is the second author's point of view about genetically changed foods?

    _____

    _____

4. What argument does the second author make to support that point of view?

    _____

    _____

B. Work with a partner. Read the passage aloud. Pay attention to phrasing. Stop after one minute. Fill out the chart.

	Words Read	–	Number of Errors	=	Words Correct Score
First Read		–		=	
Second Read		–		=	

Name _____

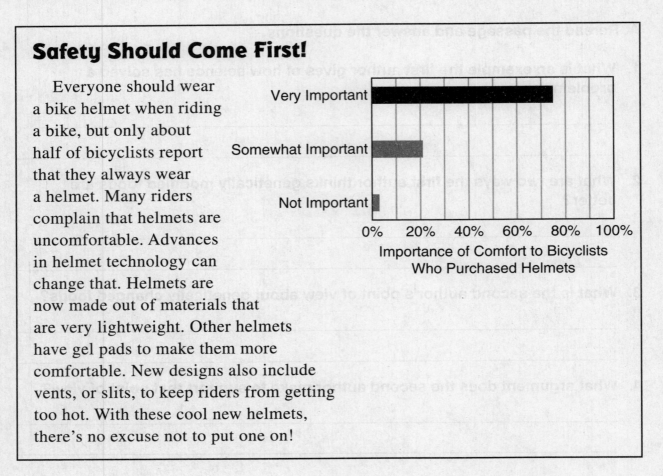

Safety Should Come First!

Everyone should wear a bike helmet when riding a bike, but only about half of bicyclists report that they always wear a helmet. Many riders complain that helmets are uncomfortable. Advances in helmet technology can change that. Helmets are now made out of materials that are very lightweight. Other helmets have gel pads to make them more comfortable. New designs also include vents, or slits, to keep riders from getting too hot. With these cool new helmets, there's no excuse not to put one on!

Very Important

Somewhat Important

Not Important

0%   20%   40%   60%   80%   100%

Importance of Comfort to Bicyclists
Who Purchased Helmets

Answer the questions about the text.

1. What is the point of view of the author of this text?

   _____

2. Name a major argument the author makes to support that point of view.

   _____

3. What is the text feature in this text? What type of information does it provide?

   _____

4. What details in the text feature support the author's argument?

   _____

   _____

   _____

Name _____

Read each passage and underline each correct word choice. Then write a definition of the word you chose.

1. Scientists have also increased the nutrition in certain crops. Such genetically modified foods can fight (malnutrition, internutrition, transnutrition).

   _____

2. Scientists have not studied the long-term results of these (ecospecies, malspecies, interspecies) changes or their effects on human health. For example, if a gene from fish were put into peas, would someone allergic to fish also be allergic to those peas?

   _____

3. Could genetically modified crops that are resistant to insects cause some insects to die off, creating an (ecobalance, imbalance, interbalance) in the (intersystem, malsystem, ecosystem)?

   _____

   _____

Name _____

A. Read each sentence. Circle the words that have the /ûr/ sound.

1. It was a perfect day to go surfing in the ocean.

2. The coach was stern, but she spurred the team to victory.

3. The dog ran in circles around the children, yearning to play.

4. I am scared about what might lurk around the corner.

5. I think that bird will pursue the flying insect.

B. Read the words in each row. Underline the two words in the row that contain the /ûr/ sound.

6. clear	spurt	engineer	swerve
7. verse	jeer	sneer	western
8. surface	dreary	tearful	squirm
9. urban	lurch	year	aboard
10. thirsty	clear	blurt	barge

Name _____

> *Evidence* is details and examples from a text that support a writer's opinion. The student who wrote the paragraph below cited evidence to show how well an author supports his or her position on a topic.
>
> **Topic sentence** → I think that the author of "The GMF Solution" does a good job of supporting his or her position. In "The GMF Solution," the author includes many facts to support the point that genetically modified foods can be helpful. The author includes the fact that scientists have added iron and Vitamin A to rice. The author also presents facts about scientists who create crops that can grow in harsh conditions and have increased harvests. These reasons and evidence support the author's points and make the author's argument convincing.
>
> **Evidence** →
>
> **Concluding statement** →

Write a paragraph about the text you have chosen. Cite evidence from the text to show how well an author supports his or her position. Remember to include a concluding statement and to use complete sentences.

Write a topic sentence: _____

_____

Cite evidence from the text: _____

_____

_____

_____

_____

End with a concluding statement: _____

_____

Name _____

A. Read the draft model. Use the questions that follow the draft to help you think about ways to vary sentence structure.

Draft Model

Our food pantry helps homeless people. Our food pantry helps families in need. Our food pantry could help even more. Our town should help the pantry.

---

1. How can you combine the first and second sentences to show how they are related? What kind of sentence could you create?

2. How could you change the structure of the third sentence to make it more specific and interesting?

3. What additional related information might make this paragraph more interesting? What kinds of sentences could you use for variety?

B. Now revise the draft by varying the sentence structure.

_____

_____

_____

_____

_____

_____

_____

_____

_____

_____

_____

_____

_____

_____

Name _____

resolve	convention	situation	union
committees	representatives	debate	proposal

Finish each sentence using the vocabulary word provided.

1. **(proposal)** She made a _____

    _____ .

2. **(debate)** The two teams will _____

    _____ .

3. **(resolve)** There is no easy way to _____

    _____ .

4. **(committees)** He serves on three _____

    _____ .

5. **(situation)** We need to talk _____

    _____ .

6. **(union)** The two groups _____

    _____ .

7. **(representatives)** The members of the council _____

    _____ .

8. **(convention)** We will enjoy going to the _____

    _____ .

Name _____

Read the selection. Complete the problem and solution graphic organizer.

Problem	Solution

Name _____

Read the passage. Use the reread strategy to make sure you understand what you have read.

The Oregon Treaty

12	The United States began on the east coast of North America. Over
22	seven decades, the country spread west. Different regions were acquired,
34	or added, at different times. By the mid-1800s, the country stretched the
38	width of the continent.
49	As it grew, the United States sometimes clashed with other countries.
61	Both the United States and Great Britain, for example, wanted the Oregon
71	Territory. Great Britain wanted the Territory for its North American
82	colony, which would later become Canada. The United States wanted the
	land for its people.

The Claims

86	
88	The Oregon Territory stretched from the Pacific Ocean to the Rocky
99	Mountains. Russian Alaska was to the north. Mexican California was to
110	the south. Part of the Territory would later become the states of Oregon,
123	Washington, and Idaho. Part of it would become the Canadian province of
135	British Columbia.
137	Both the United States and Great Britain had valid, or reasonable,
148	claims to the land. Explorers from both countries had traveled there. Both
160	countries had trading posts there.

The Conflict

165	
167	The United States and Great Britain fought each other in the War of
180	1812. At war's end in 1815, both sides kept naval ships on the Great
194	Lakes. This fed tension between the countries.
201	In 1818 the United States and Great Britain signed treaties to ease that
214	tension. One treaty designated, or chose, the 49th parallel as the border
226	between the United States and Great Britain's colony. The border stopped at
238	the Rocky Mountains. The parties could not agree on a way to split the Oregon
253	Territory. They did agree that settlers from both countries could move there.

Name _____

Settlers migrated to the Oregon Territory by the thousands. To migrate is to move from one place to another. Many used the Oregon Trail, which opened in 1843.

The presence of so many United States citizens in the Territory had a big impact. The United States felt it had to force its claim to the region. Great Britain saw that it would never rule the whole Territory. Both sides were ready to end the conflict.

The Compromise

In 1845 James Polk became president of the United States. He had used the campaign slogan, or motto, "54–40 or fight!" The 54–40 line formed the Oregon Territory's northern edge. Polk vowed that the United States would own the whole Territory. If needed, he would go to war to get it.

In the mid-1840s, the United States was close to going to war with Mexico over Texas. The United States was not strong enough to fight two wars at the same time. For economic reasons, Great Britain was not ready for war either. The two sides agreed to negotiate. To negotiate is to discuss the terms of an agreement.

Polk knew Great Britain would not give the United States the whole Oregon Territory. He proposed splitting the region at the 49th parallel. Britain would get the land north of the line. The United States would get the land south of it.

Great Britain had one condition. A border straight across the 49th parallel would divide Vancouver Island. Great Britain wanted the whole island.

Polk agreed. The Oregon Treaty of 1846 was signed. The border was set at the 49th parallel, except at Vancouver Island. There, the line curved south to give the entire island to Great Britain.

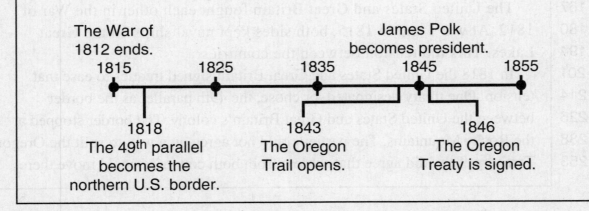

The War of 1812 ends. 1815

1825

James Polk becomes president. 1845

1835

1855

1818 The 49th parallel becomes the northern U.S. border.

1843 The Oregon Trail opens.

1846 The Oregon Treaty is signed.

Name _____

A. Reread the passage and answer the questions.

1. **Underline the words in each sentence below that are clues to a problem. Then circle the statement that best summarizes the main problem of the passage.**

   As it grew, the United States sometimes clashed with other countries.

   The United States and Great Britain fought each other in the War of 1812.

   The parties could not agree on a way to split the Oregon Territory.

2. **Write the sentence from the text that tells what President Polk said he would do to get all of the Oregon Territory.**

   _____

   _____

3. **In your own words, state the compromise that the two countries reached regarding the Oregon Territory.**

   _____

   _____

   _____

B. Work with a partner. Read the passage aloud. Pay attention to rate and accuracy. Stop after one minute. Fill out the chart.

	Words Read	–	Number of Errors	=	Words Correct Score
First Read		–		=	
Second Read		–		=	

Name _____

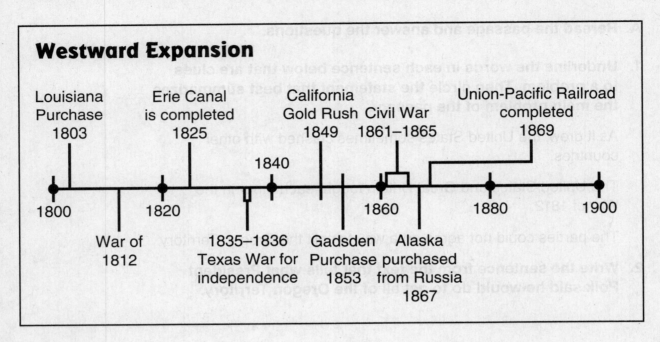

Westward Expansion

Louisiana Purchase 1803 — Erie Canal is completed 1825 — California Gold Rush 1849 — Civil War 1861–1865 — Union-Pacific Railroad completed 1869

1800 — 1820 — 1840 — 1860 — 1880 — 1900

War of 1812 — 1835–1836 Texas War for independence — Gadsden Purchase 1853 — Alaska purchased from Russia 1867

Use information from the time line to answer the questions.

1. Each dotted mark on the time line represents how many years?

_____

2. Which event took place first—the California Gold Rush or the Civil War?

_____

3. When was the Erie Canal completed?

_____

4. Which event took place later—the completion of the Erie Canal or the beginning of the Civil War?

_____

5. How much time elapsed between the Louisiana Purchase and the Gadsden Purchase?

_____

Name _____

Read each passage. Underline the context clues that help you figure out the meaning of each word in bold. Then write a new sentence using the word in bold.

1. Over seven decades, the country spread west. Different regions were **acquired**, or added, at different times.

   _____

   _____

2. Both the United States and Great Britain had **valid**, or reasonable, claims to the land.

   _____

   _____

3. One treaty **designated**, or chose, the 49th parallel as the border between the United States and Great Britain's colony.

   _____

   _____

4. Settlers **migrated** to the Oregon Territory by the thousands. To migrate is to move from one place to another.

   _____

   _____

5. The two sides agreed to **negotiate**. To negotiate is to discuss the terms of an agreement.

   _____

   _____

Name _____

bawl	because	brought	clause	counter	crawl	crowd	draw
talking	fought	foul	fountain	joint	loyal	oink	royal
saucer	thought	towel	wander	voice	town	enjoyment	wasp

A. Sort the words in the word box by the spelling of the sound. Underline the letter or letters that stand for the sound.

a as in *water* _____ _____ _____

ough as in *bought* _____ _____ _____

aw as in *saw* _____ _____ _____

au as in *pause* _____ _____ _____

oi as in *coin* _____ _____ _____

oy as in *boy* _____ _____ _____

ou as in *round* _____ _____ _____

ow as in *cow* _____ _____ _____

B. Use your completed chart to write the different ways to spell each sound.

1. Words with /ô/ such as *lawn* _____

2. Words with /oi/ such as *coin* _____

3. Words with /ou/ such as *house* _____

Name _____

> *Evidence* is details and examples from a text that support a writer's ideas. The student who wrote the paragraph below cited evidence that shows how the author uses headings to organize events.
>
> **Topic sentence** → In "The Oregon Treaty," the author uses headings to organize events that led to the Oregon Treaty. Under the heading "Claims," the author states that there was a problem with the Oregon Territory. Great Britain and the United States had claims to it. Under "Conflict" the author describes
>
> **Evidence** → the agreements and disagreements between the two countries. Under "Compromise" the author explains that President Polk came up with a solution that would split the land. Great
>
> **Concluding statement** → Britain agreed and signed the Oregon Treaty. The author uses headings to organize events that led to the Oregon Treaty.

Write a paragraph about the text you have chosen. Cite evidence to show how the author used headings to organize events or ideas.

Write a topic sentence: _____

_____

Cite evidence from the text: _____

_____

_____

_____

_____

End with a concluding statement: _____

_____

Name _____

A. Read the draft model. Use the questions that follow the draft to help you think about how you can strengthen the main idea by narrowing the focus.

Draft Model

The U.S. Constitution was important. It made sure the leaders would not have too much power. The Declaration of Independence was important too.

---

1. What is the main idea of the text?

2. What examples could be added to show how the U.S. Constitution limited leaders' power?

3. What examples would show in what other ways the Constitution was important to the country?

4. What details could be changed or removed in order to strengthen the focus on the main idea?

B. Now revise the draft by adding facts and examples that strengthen the main idea by narrowing the focus.

_____

_____

_____

_____

_____

_____

_____

Name _____

consults   presence   circumstances   unsure

consideration   destiny   expectations   reveal

Use each pair of vocabulary words in a single sentence.

1. consults, consideration

_____

_____

_____

_____

2. unsure, destiny

_____

_____

_____

_____

3. presence, circumstances

_____

_____

_____

_____

4. reveal, expectations

_____

_____

_____

_____

Name _____

Read the selection. Complete the compare and contrast graphic organizer.

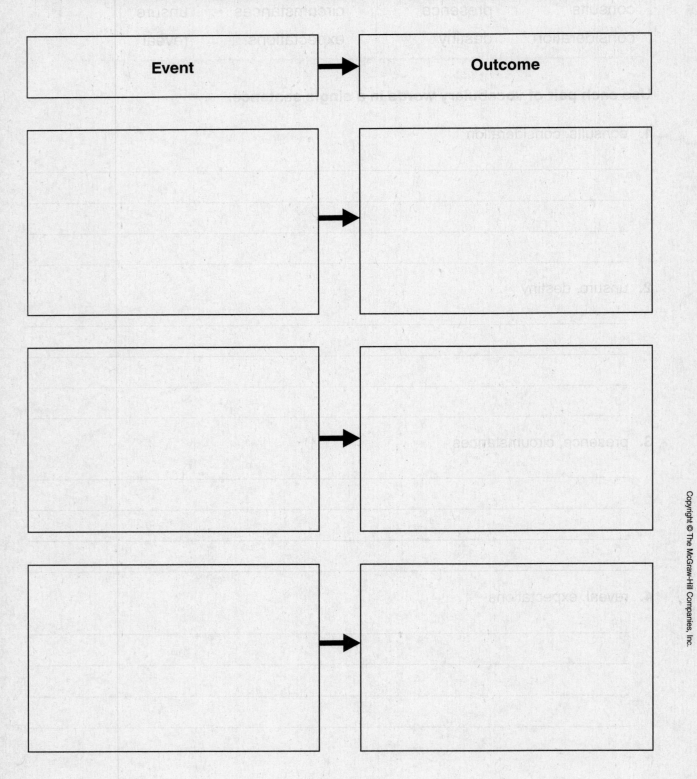

Event		Outcome

Name _____

Read the passage. Use the strategy of making, confirming, and revising predictions to check your understanding.

The Very Tiny House

	There once was a farmer and his wife who lived in a very tiny house
15	in a beautiful valley near a lovely green forest. They were as happy as a
30	king and queen working each day on their farm. They enjoyed their time
43	together. During the day they worked in the fields and cared for their
56	animals. In the evenings, they took turns preparing dinner, and afterward,
67	they would play games or make up songs to sing to each other. They
81	were two peas in a pod who liked the same things and enjoyed the same
96	activities.
97	There was one thing, however, on which they disagreed. As much as
109	she loved the farm and their beautiful surroundings, the wife felt that their
122	tiny house was too small for them. She wanted to have room for a piano
137	to accompany them on their sing-alongs. Because they both liked to cook,
149	she thought they should have a larger kitchen with a big stove and pantry
163	to store their food. "This house is a closet," she told her husband.
176	Now, the small space did not bother the farmer as much as it did his
191	wife. They had no room for a piano, but he could play guitar while they
206	sang. Although their kitchen was tiny, he was happy to barbeque outdoors.
218	However, he wanted his wife to be happy. "What can I do to get a bigger
234	house?" he asked himself.
238	The farmer thought their banker might show him how he could get a
251	larger house. He asked the banker, who said, "Let's check your savings."
263	The bank account, however, was as empty as an old tin can. There was no
278	money to buy another house.
283	Next, the farmer thought about building more rooms onto the tiny
294	house. He asked his friend the carpenter for advice. "Yes, you can do that,"
308	said his friend. With some old tools and wood from the forest, the farmer
322	began building. Now, he was good at growing crops and taking care of
335	animals, but he was not a carpenter. He thought he had built a fine wall,
350	but it crumbled like a cookie.

Name _____

The farmer was becoming discouraged. He could not buy or build a bigger house, and his wife was still unhappy. He thought and thought and worried. "What can I do? Who else can I ask?" he wondered. At last, he had another idea. He would consult Owl, the wisest creature in the forest.

So, one night the farmer crept out of the house as quietly as a mouse. He found Owl perched in the oldest tree in the forest. Owl's eyes were glowing golden jewels that gazed down at the farmer. He listened patiently to the farmer and then he gave the farmer a plan.

In the morning, the farmer brought the family's cow into the tiny house. His wife became so upset she was a storm cloud ready to rain. There was no room in the house for a cow she told him. Her husband said that the cow would be happier in the house and would give more milk. The next day, he brought in ten fat chickens. He said that they would lay more eggs inside the cozy house. On the following day, three fluffy sheep came to live in the house. Their wool would keep everyone warmer on cool nights, the farmer told his wife.

The farmer brought their cow to live inside the tiny house.

This continued until the farmer and his wife were also living with several goats and a very old horse. Hens laid eggs on the chairs and goats gobbled up the blankets.

The farmer's wife was happy with the extra eggs and gallons of milk. After several days, however, she exploded. "Our house is a shoebox!" she told her husband. He couldn't hear her because of all the noise in the animal-filled house.

Then one night, while she slept, the farmer quietly herded all of the animals out of the house and back to the barnyard. This was the last part of the plan that Owl had given him. When his wife woke up, she could not believe her eyes. The very tiny house no longer seemed tiny at all. The farmer and his wife smiled. He picked up their guitar and they sang a long and happy song.

Name _____

A. Reread the passage and answer the questions.

1. How does the farmer's interaction with Owl compare with his interactions with the banker and the carpenter?

_____

_____

_____

2. How does the wife react when the farmer starts bringing animals into the tiny house? How does she react once the animals are gone?

_____

_____

_____

3. Why does the wife's opinion of the tiny house change at the end of the story?

_____

_____

_____

B. Work with a partner. Read the passage aloud. Pay attention to expression and accuracy. Stop after one minute. Fill out the chart.

	Words Read	–	Number of Errors	=	Words Correct Score
First Read		–		=	
Second Read		–		=	

Name _____

Jack Appears

One morning, up high in the clouds, a humongous giant was taking his daily walk when, completely without warning, the tip-top of a beanstalk popped up near his feet.

"Whoa!" he exclaimed, totally startled, his voice like thunder. "Fee, Fi, Fo, Fum. Where in the world did *that* come from?"

"Hi!" a boy's voice called back through the fog, in tones of utter surprise. "My name's Jack!"

Answer the questions about the text.

1. How do you know this text is a fairy tale?

_____

_____

2. What is the setting of the text? Why is the setting important?

_____

_____

3. What do the details of the illustration tell you about the text?

_____

_____

_____

4. What visual clue does the illustration give about the giant's reaction to Jack?

_____

_____

Name _____

Read each sentence below. Write the simile or metaphor it contains and tell which it is. Then write what it means.

1. "This house is a closet," she told her husband.

   _____

   _____

2. The bank account, however, was as empty as an old tin can.

   _____

   _____

3. Owl's eyes were glowing golden jewels that gazed down at the farmer.

   _____

   _____

4. So, one night the farmer crept out of the house as quietly as a mouse.

   _____

   _____

Name _____

A. Write the plural form of each word on the line provided.

1. notch _____

2. ability _____

3. loss _____

4. rattler _____

5. tax _____

6. reptile _____

B. Write the singular form of each word on the line provided.

7. identities _____

8. lashes _____

9. beliefs _____

10. difficulties _____

11. surroundings _____

12. eddies _____

Name _____

Evidence is details and examples from a text that support a writer's ideas. The student who wrote the paragraph below cited evidence that shows how the illustration gives clues about the outcome of events.

Topic sentence ⟶ In "The Very Tiny House," the illustration gives clues to the outcome of the farmer's actions. I read that the farmer's wife is unhappy because their house is so small. The

Evidence ⟶ illustration shows the farmer walking his large cow to his tiny house. The size of the cow and the size of the house are clues that the cow will not fit in the house. This illustration helps me predict that his wife will be upset when the farmer

Concluding statement ⟶ brings the cow into the house. The illustration gives clues that the farmer's actions will cause his wife to be upset.

Write a paragraph about the text you have chosen. Cite evidence to show how an illustration at the beginning or middle of a story gives you clues to the outcome of events.

Write a topic sentence: _____

_____

Cite evidence from the text: _____

_____

_____

_____

_____

End with a concluding statement: _____

_____

Name _____

A. Read the draft model. Use the questions that follow the draft to help you think about what details you can add to create a strong opening.

Draft Model

A girl was keeping watch over the sheep. Suddenly, she had an idea. She yelled, "Help, help! A wolf is attacking the sheep!"

---

1. What details would help introduce the character of the girl? What details would help establish the setting?

2. What vivid details would grab the reader's interest?

3. What details could you add about what the girl's idea is and why she has it?

B. Now revise the draft to grab the reader's attention. Add details to help present the character in a more interesting way.

_____

_____

_____

_____

_____

_____

_____

Name _____

| behaviors | disappearance | energetic | flurry |
| migrate | observation | theory | transformed |

Write a complete sentence to answer each question below. In your answer, use the vocabulary word in bold.

1. What are some **behaviors** that are often rewarded? _____

_____

2. What might cause the **disappearance** of animals in the wild?

_____

_____

3. What kind of work would be good for an **energetic** person?

_____

_____

4. When is there a **flurry** of activity in your school? _____

_____

5. What kinds of animals **migrate** to or from the area where you live?

_____

_____

6. What is an **observation** you have made about the weather in your area?

_____

_____

7. In what school subject might you test a new **theory**?_____

_____

8. How can an actor be **transformed** in a movie?

_____

_____

Name _____

Read the selection. Complete the sequence graphic organizer.

Event

↓

↓

↓

Name _____

Read the passage. Use the reread strategy to check your understanding of new information or difficult facts.

From Slave to Scientist

10	George Washington Carver was an African American born into slavery
23	in the South. He went on to become an agricultural chemist. He also
35	taught and did research. His research made him well known, but teaching the children of former slaves may have meant more to him.

Early Years

46

48	Carver was the son of a slave woman owned by Moses Carver. As a
62	child, Carver was greatly interested in plants. When he walked in the
74	woods, he would collect different types. He loved to learn. He learned
86	to read and write when he was still a young boy. At first he was taught
102	at home. Then when he was about 11 years old, he went to a school for
118	black children.
120	For the next 20 years, Carver worked his way through school. In 1890
133	he started college. He showed skill as an artist, but he wanted a career in
148	agriculture. Carver hoped that his work would help African Americans
158	in the South. Many of them worked on farms. Carver finished college in
171	1894. Then he earned a master's degree in 1896.

Tuskegee Instructor and Researcher

180

184	Carver then moved to Alabama to teach at the Tuskegee Institute.
195	This was a school for African Americans. Carver became head of the
207	agriculture department.
209	Carver and his capable students ran experiments to test the soil in
221	Alabama. Through these tests, the students could find out which kinds of
233	plants would grow well there.

Name _____

In later years, Carver led other research projects to help southern farmers. He looked for ways that farmers could grow more crops. His teams ran experiments in soil management and crop production. He also managed an experimental farm. There his students planted different types of crops to see which ones would grow best.

The soil in many places in the South was ruined by the planting of only cotton. Cotton had been planted year after year. Carver told local farmers to plant peanuts and sweet potatoes. He found that these crops would grow well in the Alabama soil. They would also put health back into the soil.

Carver developed hundreds of foods and other products from peanuts and sweet potatoes.

Through research, Carver found that peanuts could be made into many kinds of items. He made at least 300 products from peanuts. Some of these were cheese, milk, and soap. Sweet potatoes also turned out to have many uses. Carver made more than 100 products from sweet potatoes. Flour, ink, and glue were a few of these.

In 1914 Carver published information about his research. As a result, many more farmers began to raise peanuts and sweet potatoes. In 1921 Carver spoke before Congress. He explained the value of peanut production. The peanut became a leading crop in the country. Carver freed the South from its dependence on cotton.

Later Years

In 1940, Carver gave his life savings to the Tuskegee Institute. The funds were used to create the George Washington Carver Research Foundation. Carver died in 1943. He is buried on the grounds of the Tuskegee Institute—the place where he had enjoyed such a long and rewarding career.

Name _____

A. Reread the passage and answer the questions.

1. What sequence of events might you include in a summary of George Washington Carver's education?

   _____

   _____

   _____

2. What happened *after* Carver published his research on peanuts? Tell where in the passage you found the evidence for your answer.

   _____

   _____

   _____

3. How do the subheads support the chronological sequence of the passage?

   _____

   _____

   _____

B. Work with a partner. Read the passage aloud. Pay attention to expression and phrasing. Stop after one minute. Fill out the chart.

	Words Read	−	Number of Errors	=	Words Correct Score
First Read		−		=	
Second Read		−		=	

Name _____

The Bear Facts

Frank Craighead and his twin brother John grew up near Washington, D.C. They learned a great deal about nature from their father. The brothers later used this experience to create survival courses for the military. After World War II, Frank and his brother studied grizzly bears in Yellowstone Park. Frank developed radio collars to track bears as they roamed from place to place. His observations made him an expert on bear behavior.

Frank Craighead studied grizzly bears. He helped protect their habitat.

Answer the questions about the text.

1. **How can you tell that this text is a biography?**

_____

_____

2. **What evidence from the text suggests that Frank Craighead thought of new ways to study wildlife?**

_____

_____

3. **How are the events from Frank Craighead's life presented in the text?**

_____

_____

4. **What additional information does the photo caption provide about Frank Craighead?**

_____

_____

Name _____

Underline the word in each sentence that contains a Greek or Latin suffix. Then write your own sentence using the word correctly.

1. George Washington Carver went on to become a chemist.

_____

_____

2. Carver showed skill as an artist, but he wanted a career in agriculture.

_____

_____

3. Carver's teams studied methods of soil management.

_____

_____

4. Carver freed the South from its dependence on cotton.

_____

_____

5. In 1914 Carver published information about his research.

_____

_____

Name _____

A. Write the correct *-ed* and *-ing* forms of each verb.

Verb	+ *ed*	+ *ing*
1. regret	_____	_____
2. amuse	_____	_____
3. qualify	_____	_____
4. ease	_____	_____
5. threaten	_____	_____

B. Add the correct *-ed* or *-ing* ending to the verb in parentheses to complete each sentence. When the action happens is shown.

6. *now* The thin paint is **(drip)** _____ down the canvas.

7. *past* The new bird species **(fascinate)** _____ the young biologist.

8. *past* My mother **(study)** _____ books about unusual animals.

9. *now* The camping store is **(donate)** _____ supplies for our trip.

10. *now* We are **(hope)** _____ to see many natural wonders.

Name _____

> *Evidence* is details and examples from a text that support a writer's opinion. The student who wrote the paragraph below cited evidence that supports the opinion that the author did a good job of putting events in sequence.
>
> **Topic sentence** →   I think that the author of "From Slave to Scientist" does a good job of putting the events of George Washington Carver's life in sequence. Under "Early Years," the author
>
> **Evidence** → describes Carver's childhood and studies. In the next section, the author describes Carver's work as a teacher and researcher. In the last section, the author explains that Carver gave money to the Tuskegee Institute before he died. The author includes dates and the sequence words "at first,"
>
> **Concluding statement** → "then," and "in later years." The author does a good job of showing the sequence of events in Carver's life.

Write a paragraph about the text you have chosen. Tell how well the author organized events in sequence. Cite evidence to support your opinion.

Write a topic sentence: _____

_____

Cite evidence from the text: _____

_____

_____

_____

_____

End with a concluding statement: _____

_____

Name _____

A. Read the draft model. Use the questions that follow the draft to help you think about what details you can add to support the main idea.

Draft Model

Cacti need special care. They aren't like other plants. I looked it up, and I found out how to care for them.

---

1. What facts, examples, and concrete details would help readers understand what kind of care cacti need?

2. What details would help explain how cacti are not like other plants?

3. What other details would help develop the main idea and make it more interesting?

B. Now revise the draft by adding details to help support the main idea.

_____

_____

_____

_____

_____

_____

_____

_____

Name _____

| assuring | pursuit | gratitude | emerging |
| detected | previous | outcome | guidance |

Finish each sentence using the vocabulary word provided.

1. **(gratitude)** He expressed _____

_____.

2. **(guidance)** She learned how _____

_____.

3. **(assuring)** Before the play, the drama teacher _____

_____.

4. **(outcome)** I can predict _____

_____.

5. **(previous)** I remember _____

_____.

6. **(pursuit)** The dog ran quickly _____

_____.

7. **(detected)** When I looked under the porch, _____

_____.

8. **(emerging)** We saw a deer _____

_____.

Name _____

Read the selection. Complete the theme graphic organizer.

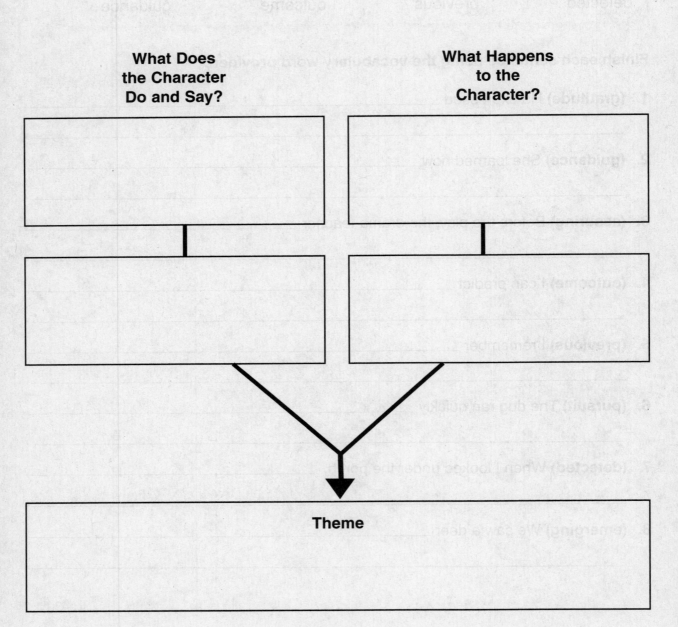

Name _____

Read the passage. Use the make, confirm, and revise predictions strategy
to help you set a purpose for reading and to understand what you read.

How the Fly Saved the River

	When the world was young, a long river wandered through a large
12	forest. It offered its water freely to anyone who needed it.
23	Fish of all shapes and sizes lived in the river. Beavers built their dams
37	and lodges in it. Muskrats swam there and built nests in its banks. Other
51	animals visited the river. Bears, deer, birds, and even insects drank the
63	delicious water and gossiped while relaxing among the sheltering trees on
74	the river's shores.
77	One day, a giant moose heard about the river and how delicious and
90	refreshing its water was. He decided to travel there and sample the
102	water himself. When he arrived, the moose was extremely thirsty and
113	immediately began to drink. Even after he quenched his thirst, the moose
125	kept drinking. He decided he wanted all the water for himself. The other
138	animals watched in horror. The moose was drinking so much the water was
151	sinking! The more the moose drank, the more the water retreated.
162	The farther the river sank, the more the animals worried. "What will we
175	drink?" asked the bear. "Where will we relax in the cool shade?" wondered
188	the deer. The muskrats worried, too. Where would they swim and play?
200	The beavers were even more worried. Where would they build their dams
212	and their lodges? The fish were the most worried of all, desperately
224	complaining to the other animals, "What if the river dries up? We can't
237	live on land like you!"
242	That night, the animals convened a meeting to figure out a way to keep
256	the greedy moose from drinking the river. The moose was so huge and so
270	strong that they were all afraid of him. The bear exclaimed, "Have you
283	seen his antlers? They're almost as gigantic as he is!" and he trembled as
297	he said it.
300	Then the silence was broken by a small voice: "I'll do it." The animals
314	turned, wondering who this courageous creature might be.

Name _____

It was the fly. Despite their fear, the animals burst out laughing. "What a ridiculous idea!" the bear told the fly, "You're too small. You can't chase away such a big animal! Why, even I am afraid of him!"

"Someone has to stop him," said the fly, "and none of you are willing to try." With that, she flew off to make a plan.

The next morning the moose returned to the river and started drinking greedily. He didn't notice the fly hovering above him, selecting her first target. Suddenly, out of the sky she dove, landing on his leg and sinking her jaws into it. The moose stamped his foot, trying to throw her off, but the fly held on tight. He kept stamping his foot, and with every stamp, he left a hole in the ground. The river hurried to fill the holes. Soon, mud was grabbing at the moose's feet. Next, the fly landed on the moose's back. Again, she bit as hard as she could. The moose tossed his head, snapping at the fly. All he managed to do, though, was give himself some nasty scratches with his antlers. Then, the fly started a series of quick attacks. She darted in from one side to nip the moose's ear and then from the other to bite his nose.

The moose galloped frantically back and forth on the river bank, snapping wildly at the fly with his massive jaws. He thrashed his head from side to side and stamped his hooves so hard the ground shook. He snorted like thunder and blew like a hurricane. No matter what he did, though, he couldn't get rid of the little fly.

At last, the moose stopped fighting and started running. The fly pursued him, buzzing loudly. When she was sure he wasn't coming back, she finally flew home.

At the river, the other animals crowded around to thank her for banishing the moose. "The moose couldn't fight someone as small as you," the bear said. "By using your brain, you figured out a way to turn your weakness into a strength."

Name _____

A. Reread the passage and answer the questions.

1. When the animals hold a meeting about the moose, what do they say and do?

_____

_____

_____

2. What does the fly do after the meeting? How do the animals react?

_____

_____

_____

3. What is the message of this story?

_____

_____

_____

B. Work with a partner. Read the passage aloud. Pay attention to rate. Stop after one minute. Fill out the chart.

	Words Read	–	Number of Errors	=	Words Correct Score
First Read		–		=	
Second Read		–		=	

Name _____

The Hunter and the Doves

A flock of doves rested under a banyan tree, calmly eating grains of rice. Suddenly, a hunter's net descended and trapped them. The king of doves made an escape plan, "We will fly up together, clutching the net in our beaks. There is strength in unity. When we are safe from pursuit, we will find a way to get free from the net." The doves flew away from the hunter, clutching the net in their beaks. The king guided them to the home of his friend, the mouse. Mouse was known for helping others. The mouse nibbled the net and freed the doves. The doves expressed their gratitude to the mouse for his help and flew away.

Answer the questions about the text.

1. **How do you know this is a folktale?**

_____

_____

2. **What example of foreshadowing does this text include?**

_____

_____

3. **What lesson does the text contain?**

_____

_____

4. **What example of imagery does the text include? What is the effect of this imagery?**

_____

_____

Name _____

Read each passage. Underline the word or words that show personification. Then write a sentence about the mental picture you have of the thing described.

1. When the world was young, a long river wandered through a large forest.

   _____

   _____

2. The river offered its water freely to anyone who needed it.

   _____

   _____

3. The more the moose drank, the more the water retreated.

   _____

   _____

4. The river hurried to fill the holes.

   _____

   _____

5. Soon, mud was grabbing at the moose's feet.

   _____

   _____

Name _____

A. Write the words each contraction stands for.

1. you're   _____

2. what's   _____

3. wasn't   _____

4. shouldn't _____

5. there's   _____

6. didn't   _____

7. doesn't   _____

8. we're   _____

B. Circle the letter or letters left out of each contraction.

9. that's	es	i	is
10. we've	ive	ave	ha
11. don't	o	it	not
12. they're	are	a	i
13. couldn't	nt	o	t
14. he'd	ha	a	h

Name _____

> *Evidence* is details and examples from a text that support a writer's ideas. The student who wrote the paragraph below cited evidence that shows how the author uses repetition to convey the theme, or main message.
>
> **Topic sentence** ⟶   In "How the Fly Saved the River," the author uses the repetition of the fly's actions to convey the message that courage and determination give you strength. The small fly
>
> **Evidence** ⟶ decides to stop the giant moose from drinking all the water. She bites the moose over and over. The moose snaps at the fly, but the fly bites the moose again and again. The moose runs away, but the fly pursues the moose. The repetition
>
> **Concluding statement** ⟶ of these actions conveys the message that courage and determination can give you strength.

Write a paragraph about the text you have chosen. Cite evidence from the text to show how the author uses repetition to convey a theme, or message.

Write a topic sentence: _____

_____

Cite evidence from the text: _____

_____

_____

_____

_____

End with a concluding statement: _____

_____

Name _____

A. Read the draft model. Use the questions that follow the draft to help you think about what details you can add or change to make the story clear and easy to follow.

Draft Model

Cinderella has many features of a folktale. The fairy godmother does magic, like many folktales. We meet the good Cinderella and her wicked stepmother. Many folktales have a good and a wicked character.

---

1. What sequence words and phrases could be added to make events easier to follow?

2. How could sentences or ideas be rearranged to help logically organize the text?

3. What other changes could be made to improve the text's flow?

B. Now revise the draft by adding words and rearranging sentences as necessary to make the story clear and easy to understand.

Name _____

| memorized | shuddered | ambitious | satisfaction |

Write a complete sentence to answer each question below. Use the vocabulary word in bold.

1. Why might a student be proud if he or she **memorized** a famous speech?

   _____

   _____

2. What might it mean if you **shuddered** while reading a story?

   _____

   _____

3. What is an example of an **ambitious** project?

   _____

   _____

4. Why might someone feel **satisfaction** after completing a difficult report?

   _____

   _____

Name _____

Read the selection. Complete the theme graphic organizer.

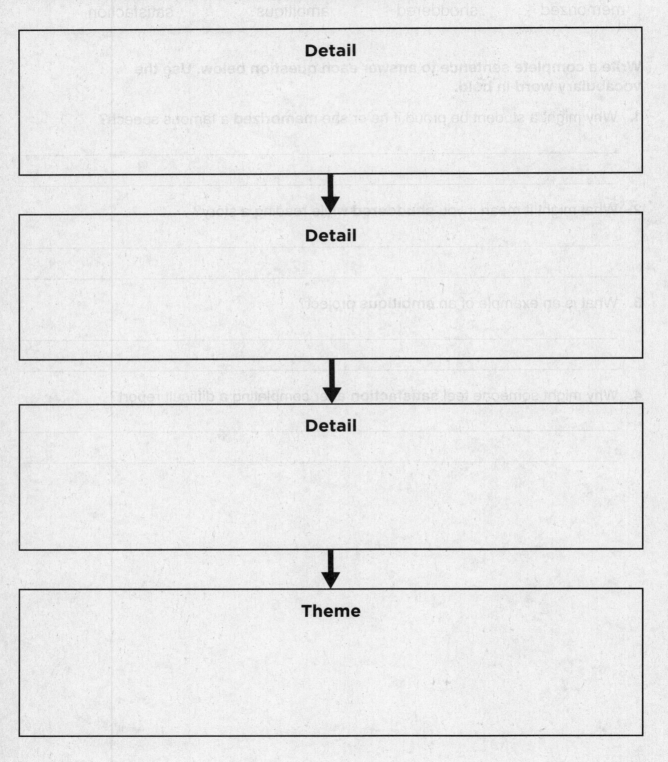

Detail

Detail

Detail

Theme

Name _____

Read the passage. As you read, ask yourself what message the author might want you to hear.

Blue Ribbon Dreams

	Five a.m., I'm out of bed,
6	Trudging to the barn, feet like lead.
13	*Training, training every day,*
17	*County fair, I'm on my way!*
23	By the entrance hangs a bit,
29	A jingling bridle next to it.
35	I wind my way back to the stall
43	"Morning, Little Red," I softly call.
49	As always, he entrances me,
54	How lovely one young horse can be!
61	Red and I are not too tall.
68	(In fact, we're really rather small).
74	Some folks, neither fair nor wise,
80	Might judge us simply by our size.
87	But I intend to demonstrate
92	That small things can be truly great.
99	So every morning, and again at night
106	I train Little Red with all my might.
114	Again, again, and yet again
119	I lead him all 'round the pen.
126	I feel Red's muscles coiled and strong.
133	Raising my head, I break out in song
141	*Training, training every day,*
145	*County fair, we're on our way.*
151	I imagine us at the county fair
158	And think of all who'll see us there.
166	Will we win? Who can know?
172	I shrug, laugh. Blue ribbon or no,
179	Today I'm 10 feet tall, Red's 20 hands high.
188	We're champions, Little Red and I.

Name _____

A. Reread the poem and answer the questions.

1. When and why does the speaker in the poem get out of bed and go to the barn?

_____

_____

2. What important event is coming soon? How do you know?

_____

_____

3. How do you think the speaker will probably feel if her horse does not win a blue ribbon?

_____

_____

4. What is the theme of the poem?

_____

_____

B. Work with a partner. Read the passage aloud. Pay attention to expression and phrasing. Stop after one minute. Fill out the chart.

	Words Read	–	Number of Errors	=	Words Correct Score
First Read		–		=	
Second Read		–		=	

Name _____

Sammy's Day Out

Sammy the wolf cub lifted his head,
And looked at the litter-mates sharing his bed.
They were all sleeping, the way youngsters ought.
So he got up, quite quietly (lest he be caught).

He crept from the bedroom, and then down the hall.
He crept down the stairs, making no sound at all.
He crept to the fridge for a big junky snack.
(In his head, his mom scolded, "Your fangs will get plaque!")

He munched, munched, and munched, and he thought and he planned,
All the ways he might spend the free time now at hand,
With no one to scold him, or tell him "Behave!"
Or "Don't chase your tail, son!" or "Go clean your cave!"

But the junk food he wolfed down soon made him feel drowsy.
And worse than that even, his stomach felt lousy.
He went to his parents, though he knew what they'd say:
"That's what you get for eating in the middle of the day!"

Answer the questions about the text.

1. **How do you know that this is narrative poetry?**

_____

2. **Name literary elements that the writer uses in this text. Give an example of each.**

_____

_____

_____

3. **What would be different about this text if it were lyric poetry?**

_____

Name _____

> **Repetition** is the repeated use of a word or phrase. Authors use repetition to emphasize an idea.
>
> **Rhyme** is the repetition of a vowel sound. Authors often use rhyme at the ends of pairs of lines or alternating lines of a poem.

**Read these two excerpts from the narrative poem "Blue Ribbon Dreams."
Then answer the questions.**

Five a.m., I'm out of bed,
Trudging to the barn, feet like lead.
  Training, training every day,
  County fair, I'm on my way!
By the entrance hangs a bit,
A jingling bridle next to it.

Again, again, and yet again
I lead him all 'round the pen.
I feel Red's muscles coiled and strong.
Raising my head, I break out in song
  Training, training every day,
  County fair, we're on our way.

---

1. **Find at least two examples of repetition in the excerpts. Write them below.**

   _____

   _____

2. **What are two examples of rhyme that appear in the excerpts?**

   _____

3. **What idea does the repetition and rhyme of the poem help express?**

   _____

   _____

Name _____

Read each pair of passages. Then, on the line below each pair, give the two definitions of the homographs in bold.

1. Trudging to the barn, feet like **lead**

   I **lead** him all 'round the pen

   _____

   _____

2. *County **fair**, I'm on my way!*

   Some folks, neither **fair** nor wise

   _____

   _____

3. By the **entrance** hangs a bit

   As always, he **entrances** me

   _____

   _____

4. **Might** judge us simply by our size

   I train Little Red with all my **might**

   _____

   _____

Name _____

A. Read the words in each row. Underline the word that has two closed syllables.

1. kennel   easy   local

2. empire   diary   dentist

3. hungry   flatter   lazy

4. summon   sameness   mainly

5. submit   retire   student

B. Divide the words into syllables by writing each syllable on the lines. Then circle the syllables that are closed syllables.

6. jogger   _____   _____

7. valley   _____   _____

8. culture   _____   _____

9. eager   _____   _____

10. pigment   _____   _____

Name _____

> *Evidence* is details and examples from a text that support a writer's ideas. The student who wrote the paragraph below cited evidence to support his or her opinion about how well two poets used precise language.
>
> **Topic sentence** → I think the poet of "Blue Ribbon Dreams" did a better job of using precise language than the poet of "Sammy's Day Out." In "Blue Ribbon Dreams," the poet uses the words "trudging" and "feet like lead." These words help me picture how the speaker walked. In "Sammy's Day Out," the poet uses the words "big junky snack." I can't picture how big the snack is or why the snack is junky. The poet's use of precise language in "Blue Ribbon Dreams" creates clearer pictures in my mind than the words the poet used in "Sammy's Day Out."
>
> **Evidence** →
>
> **Concluding statement** →

Write a paragraph about two poems. Compare how well the poets use precise language. Tell which poet did a better job. Cite details that created a picture in your mind.

Write a topic sentence: _____

_____

Cite evidence from the text: _____

_____

_____

_____

_____

End with a concluding statement: _____

_____

Name _____

A. Read the draft model. Use the questions that follow the draft to help you think about what precise language you can add.

Draft Model

Dirty dishes are piled
In the kitchen.
Time to clean!

---

1. What kinds of dishes do you imagine when you read the first line?

2. What words would help readers visualize the kitchen?

3. What vivid language would help make the scene come to life?

B. Now revise the draft by putting precise language into the description.

_____

_____

_____

_____

_____

_____

_____

Name _____

| misunderstanding | contradicted | complimenting | congratulate |
| critical | blurted | appreciation | cultural |

Finish each sentence using the vocabulary word provided.

1. **(congratulate)** If she wins the election, _____

_____.

2. **(appreciation)** I received this gift _____

_____.

3. **(complimenting)** He spends too much time _____

_____.

4. **(cultural)** The holiday we celebrate is _____

_____.

5. **(misunderstanding)** The two friends were unhappy because _____

_____.

6. **(critical)** Some people are _____

_____.

7. **(blurted)** Before he realized what he was saying, _____

_____.

8. **(contradicted)** What she said _____

_____.

Name _____

Read the selection. Complete the theme graphic organizer.

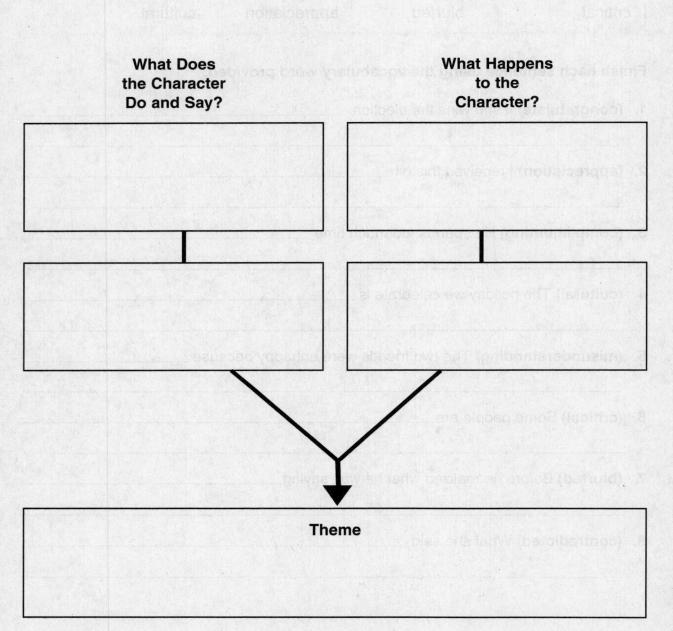

**What Does
the Character
Do and Say?**

**What Happens
to the
Character?**

Theme

Name _____

Read the passage. Use the summarizing strategy to make sure you understand what you have read.

Potluck or Potlatch?

	Alex wasn't ready to go into the house. "Are you sure that I'm supposed
14	to bring something to eat?" he asked his mother, eyeing the plate of
27	brownies in his lap. "Yuma told me I didn't have to bring anything."
40	Mrs. Martin nodded. "The purpose of a potluck is for everyone to come
53	together and share food," she reassured him, patting his leg. "Have a good
66	time, sweetie."
68	Alex exited the car and waved good-bye to his mother. Two weeks
80	ago at the bus stop, Yuma had given Alex a bundle of sticks wrapped in
95	colorful ribbons strung with beads. Yuma explained that his family was
106	hosting a potluck in honor of his new baby sister, and the sticks were a
121	traditional Native American invitation. Alex was flattered that he had
131	been invited, but he was also nervous because he had never been to a
145	potluck before.
147	Yuma greeted Alex at the door and Alex gave him the plate of brownies.
161	"What are these for?" Yuma asked, looking puzzled. He glanced up at his
174	mother, who had come over to say hello.
182	Alex looked down at his feet, embarrassed. "They're, um, for
192	the potluck," he said hesitantly. He had never felt so mortified in his
205	entire life.
207	Mrs. Wright placed a warm hand on Alex's shoulder, which made him
219	feel a little less nervous. He looked into her smiling face; she was short,
233	just about his height. "What a lovely thought," she said. "I think there may
247	have been a miscommunication, though. We're having a potlatch today, not
258	a potluck."
260	Alex didn't know what to say.

Name _____

Mrs. Wright laughed gently. "It's a common mistake," she said. "*Potluck* and *potlatch* sound a lot alike, don't they? A potlatch is a traditional celebration of our people, the Kwakiutl. The difference is that the hosts share food and gifts with the guests, not the other way around."

Alex looked around; there had to be at least a hundred people inside the house. "You're going to give gifts to all of these people?"

Alex learns that a potlatch is very different from a potluck.

Yuma's face lit up. "We've been working on gifts for months! Come see them!" He grabbed Alex's sleeve and dragged him across the room to a large table overflowing with packages. "My mother and aunts have been weaving blankets and beading jewelry since before the baby was born. I made bracelets." Yuma held out his wrist to show Alex soft strips of finely braided leather.

Alex still looked confused, so Yuma explained that the Kwakiutl people believe that wealth should be shared. Potlatches are held to honor important events, like births or marriages. A potlatch starts with a huge feast, which is followed by storytelling and traditional dances. A family works for years to save money for a potlatch, all so they can give it to friends. "To us," Yuma finished, "true wealth comes from giving, not having."

Alex considered this. "I think that's pretty cool," he said, a smile spreading across his face.

Yuma grinned back. "I do, too."

The feast was delicious, and Alex was having so much fun that he lost track of time. He was startled to see his mother at the front door because he felt as if she had just dropped him off. Alex wasn't ready to go home; the dancing and storytelling were about to start. He was relieved to see Mrs. Wright take his mother's coat. Mrs. Martin stood in the entryway, looking nervous. Alex could tell that she felt out of place, so he went over and took her hand. "Can we stay?" he asked. She nodded, a smile playing on her lips. Grinning, he eagerly led his mother to the table. He couldn't wait to tell her all about the potlatch.

Name _____

A. Reread the passage and answer the questions.

1. How does Alex feel when he arrives at Yuma's house?

_____

_____

2. Why does he feel that way?

_____

_____

3. What does Alex learn from his experience? What might be the theme, or message, of this story?

_____

_____

_____

B. Work with a partner. Read the passage aloud. Pay attention to intonation. Stop after one minute. Fill out the chart.

	Words Read	–	Number of Errors	=	Words Correct Score
First Read		–		=	
Second Read		–		=	

Name _____

The Wedding

Cindy's oldest sister, Becca, went to a wedding last weekend. Becca is telling Cindy about her friend's wedding traditions.

"The ceremony took place beneath a chuppa."

"What is a chuppa?" Cindy asked.

"A chuppa is an open tent, which stands for a new home. Then the groom gave the bride a solid gold ring, which stands for the hope that they will be together always," Becca said. "Finally, they had a party and danced a special dance called the Hora."

"That sounds like a great wedding!" exclaimed Cindy.

Answer the questions about the text.

1. **How do you know this text is realistic fiction?**

   _____

   _____

2. **Write one example of realistic dialogue found in the text. Explain why it is realistic.**

   _____

   _____

3. **How does Becca describe the chuppa and what it stands for?**

   _____

4. **Write another descriptive detail from the text. How does this detail help you experience the text as realistic?**

   _____

   _____

Name _____

Read each passage. Underline the context clues that help you figure out the meaning of each word in bold. Then tell what the word means.

1. Mrs. Wright placed a warm hand on Alex's shoulder, which made him feel a little less **nervous**.

   _____

   _____

2. Alex still looked **confused**, so Yuma explained that the Kwakiutl people believe that wealth should be shared.

   _____

   _____

3. He was **startled** to see his mother at the front door because he felt as if she had just dropped him off.

   _____

   _____

Name _____

A. Read each word. Then write each word using a slanted line (/) to divide it into syllables. Circle the open syllables.

	Syllables
1. local	_____
2. comet	_____
3. decent	_____
4. panic	_____
5. humor	_____
6. linen	_____
7. shiver	_____
8. vacant	_____
9. profile	_____
10. closet	_____
11. punish	_____
12. smoky	_____

B. Write a sentence using at least two of the words above with a V/CV syllable pattern.

_____

_____

Name _____

Evidence is details and examples from a text that support a writer's opinion. The student who wrote the paragraph below cited evidence that supports his or her opinion about how well two authors developed realistic characters.

Topic sentence →   I think the author of "Potluck or Potlatch?" did a better job of making the main character seem realistic than the author of "A Reluctant Traveler." In "Potluck or Potlatch?"

Evidence → Alex is nervous about an event he hasn't been to before. He is embarrassed when he finds out he should not have brought a dish. I think that is how most people would feel. In "A Reluctant Traveler," some details about Paul are not very realistic. He doesn't think it is fun to go on vacation to another country or city. I think most people would think it would be fun. The details the author used in "Potluck or

Concluding statement → Potlatch?" make Alex a more realistic character than Paul in "A Reluctant Traveler."

Write a paragraph about two stories you have chosen. Compare how well the authors developed realistic characters. Give your opinion about which character is the most realistic. Cite evidence from the text to support your opinion.

Write a topic sentence: _____

_____

Cite evidence from the texts: _____

_____

_____

_____

End with a concluding statement: _____

_____

Name _____

A. Read the draft model. Use the questions that follow the draft to help you think about how to revise the draft to make the voice more informal.

Draft Model

My relatives and I celebrate Thanksgiving as if it were a family reunion. Every member of my family attends. We all cook, eat, and spend time together.

---

1. How could sentences be shortened or rearranged to make them less formal?

2. What formal vocabulary could be removed? What everyday vocabulary could be added?

3. What contractions could be added?

B. Now revise the draft by adding or changing details to make the voice more informal.

_____

_____

_____

_____

_____

_____

_____

Name _____

tormentors	fashioned	shortage	devise
civilization	complex	resourceful	cultivate

Write a complete sentence to answer each question below. In your answer, use the vocabulary word in bold.

1. What is a common obstacle that every **civilization** must face?

_____

_____

2. What is something you **fashioned** with your own hands?

_____

_____

3. Why is it important for farmers to **cultivate** their land?

_____

_____

4. What would happen if there was a **shortage** of books at the library?

_____

_____

5. What is a **complex** problem that you helped solve? _____

_____

6. How would you **devise** a plan for eating better? _____

_____

7. How can dogs be **tormentors** to cats? _____

_____

8. Why would it be helpful to have a **resourceful** person as a friend?

_____

_____

Name _____

Read the selection. Complete the theme graphic organizer.

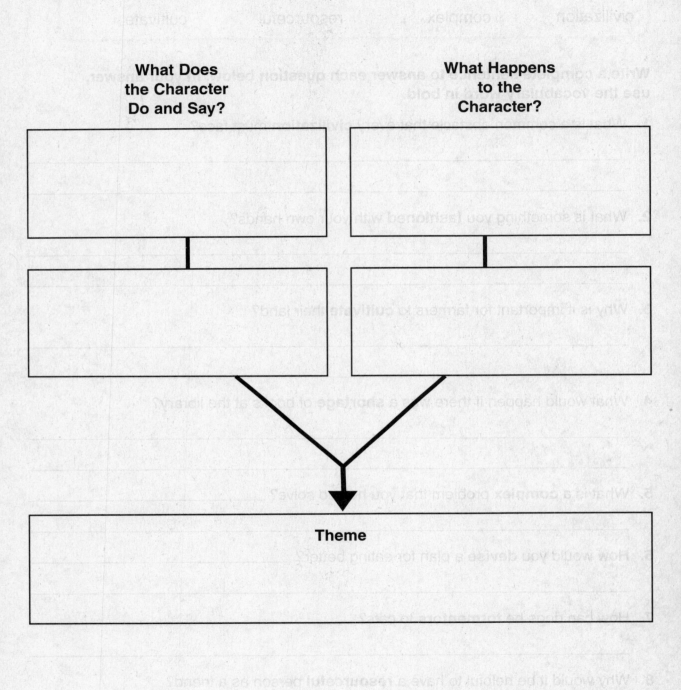

What Does
the Character
Do and Say?

What Happens
to the
Character?

Theme

Name _____

Read the passage. Use the summarizing strategy to make sure you understand what you have read.

The Cup that Shines at Night

	Ann's eyes fluttered open and she found herself lying in a moonlit
12	grassy field by her friend Mia who was slowly waking up.
23	"Where are we?" Mia asked groggily. "How did we get here?"
34	"I don't know," Ann replied. "I wonder how we'll get home."
45	An odd purple house with a crooked front door stood nearby. Spying a
58	note tacked to the door, Ann got up and pried it loose. It read: "The cup
74	that shines at night will show the way home."
83	"What in the world is the cup that shines at night?" asked Mia.
96	"Do you think maybe it's inside this weird-looking house?"
105	As if the house understood them, the door creaked open. Creeping
116	inside, they saw a table whose surface was covered with all kinds of cups.
130	A tall crystal cup waited to be filled with water. A hefty mug sat next to a
147	delicate china coffee cup, making it appear even more fragile. Towering
158	over the others was a polished silver cup. It looked like the trophy Ann had
173	won in the school science fair.
179	Puzzled, they went outside and collapsed on the porch. They had seen
191	dozens of cups, but none of them was shining. Mia asked if Ann thought
205	they'd ever get home.
209	As she considered Mia's question, Ann sighed sadly. She gazed at the
221	moonlit sky, hoping desperately that an answer might suddenly appear
231	above them.
233	Then she leapt up, gesturing eagerly skyward. "Look, it's the Big
244	Dipper! A dipper is a kind of cup, and that dipper is certainly shining! The
259	Big Dipper is made up of seven stars!"
267	"How will the Big Dipper help us get home?" demanded Mia.
278	Ann explained that drawing a line through the two stars at the front of
292	the dipper leads to Polaris, the North Star.
300	"I'll bet that's what the note means," she exclaimed. "We should let
312	Polaris lead us home."

Name _____

Keeping their eyes glued to Polaris, they started walking north. Soon they found themselves on the steep banks of a wide, rolling river. There was no visible means of getting across.

Ann and Mia believed following Polaris, the North Star, would help them find their way home.

Ann wondered it they had made a mistake. Then she spotted a scrap of paper beside the road. Another note, it read: "The wrongly named bird will carry you across."

Mia knew several different types of birds, such as cardinals, seagulls, and hummingbirds. However, she believed none of them was wrongly named. What could be the meaning of the note?

Then, from the shadows, a bat flapped silently toward them. Mia turned to run away. She had heard that bats were blind and got tangled in people's hair.

Ann told her that many bats can see as well as people can. They can also find their way by using echoes.

By this time, the bat had vanished quietly in the distance.

Rounding a curve in the road, they discovered an old covered wooden bridge. A weathered sign said "Bald Eagle River Bridge."

"That's it!" cried Ann. "The bald eagle is a wrongly named bird! It isn't bald at all. Its body is covered in brown feathers and it has white feathers on its head. The contrast makes it look bald."

Mia doubtfully eyed the ancient bridge. However, Ann grinned confidently. She was sure the bridge was their route home, and reminded Mia that they would have missed it if she had run away from the bat.

They raced eagerly over the bridge. On the other side stood their houses gleaming coldly in the moonlight.

Mia wondered why they hadn't noticed the bridge before.

"I don't know," mused Ann. "Maybe it's because we're . . ."

Suddenly her eyes popped open, and she found herself in her suburban backyard as the sun began climbing over the horizon. Snoring at a tremendous volume, Mia lay twitching, then shuddered, and struggled to sit up. Wearing a dazed expression she stammered, "I just had the strangest dream!"

Name _____

A. Reread the passage and answer the questions.

1. How does Ann figure out the meaning of the first note, "The cup that shines at night will show the way home"?

_____

_____

_____

2. How does Ann figure out the meaning of the second note, "The wrongly named bird will carry you across"?

_____

_____

3. What might be the theme, or message, of this story?

_____

_____

B. Work with a partner. Read the passage aloud. Pay attention to expression and phrasing. Stop after one minute. Fill out the chart.

	Words Read	–	Number of Errors	=	Words Correct Score
First Read		–		=	
Second Read		–		=	

Name _____

The Kingfisher Train

Kellen entered "1964 Japan bullet train" on the touchpad. It blinked and suddenly Kellen was taken back to the studio of Hideo Shima. He floated, invisible, above Hideo's drawing board. Kellen was thrilled to see his favorite inventor at work. On it was a sketch of a bullet train and a kingfisher, diving for fish. Hideo said, "When the train leaves a tunnel at over 300 kilometers per hour, it creates a shock wave that booms like thunder. Residents don't like the noise." Hideo continued, "I'll change the train's shape to mimic the kingfisher's long, thin beak. It will move quietly. Now technology and Nature will work together."

Answer the questions about the text.

1. **How do you know this text is fantasy?**

    _____

    _____

2. **Describe the setting of this text.**

    _____

    _____

3. **Find two examples of sensory language in the text. What sense does each involve?**

    _____

    _____

4. **How does the author use personification in the text?**

    _____

    _____

Name _____

Read each passage. Underline the word or phrase that completes the comparison with the word in bold. Then write the meaning of the word in bold on the line.

1. A **hefty** mug sat next to a delicate china coffee cup, making it appear even more fragile.

   hefty: _____

2. "The **bald** eagle is a wrongly named bird! It isn't bald at all. Its body is covered in brown feathers and it has white feathers on its head."

   bald: _____

3. Mia **doubtfully** eyed the ancient bridge. However, Ann grinned confidently. She was sure the bridge was their route home, and reminded Mia that they would have missed it if she had run away from the bat.

   doubtfully: _____

Name _____

A. Read the words in each row. Underline the word with the V/V pattern. Then circle the vowels that form the V/V pattern.

1.	treat	trial	train
2.	diary	distant	dairy
3.	gentle	genuine	gemstone
4.	meander	mean	mention
5.	flood	float	fluid

B. Read each word. Draw a slanted line (/) between the two vowels that form the V/V pattern. Then write the sound of the first vowel in the pattern.

6. riot _____

7. casual _____

8. meteor _____

9. diet _____

10. ideas _____

Name _____

> *Evidence* is details and examples from a text that support a writer's opinion. The student who wrote the paragraph below cited evidence that supports his or her opinion about a story event.
>
> **Topic sentence** ⟶   I think the most important event in "The Cup that Shines at Night" is when Ann looks up at the sky and sees the Big Dipper. At the beginning of the story, Ann and Mia are in a grassy field and wonder how they will get home. They find a clue that tells them "the cup that shines at night will show the way home." Ann sees the Big Dipper and figures out that
>
> **Evidence** ⟶
>
> **Concluding statement** ⟶ they can find their way home by the stars. I think this event is the most important because it begins their journey home.

Write a paragraph about the text you have chosen. Give your opinion about the most important event in the story. Cite evidence to support your opinion.

Write a topic sentence: _____

_____

Cite evidence from the text: _____

_____

_____

_____

End with a concluding statement: _____

_____

Name _____

A. Read the draft model. Use the questions that follow the draft to help you think about what words you can add to show how Sam feels about the setting.

Draft Model

Sam awoke to the sound of waves. He felt the sun on his skin, and he tasted oranges. He smelled trees.

---

1. What words can you add to the first sentence to help the reader understand how pleasant the sound of waves is?

2. What words can you add to tell how the sun feels on Sam's skin?

3. Why does he taste oranges? What words describe the taste?

4. What positive words can be added to describe the trees?

B. Now revise the draft by adding words to show how Sam feels about the setting.

Name _____

particles   contact   moisture   visible

structure   erode   formation   repetition

Finish each sentence using the vocabulary word provided.

1. **(moisture)** On a rainy day I can _____

_____.

2. **(repetition)** She learned how to _____

_____.

3. **(erode)** Wind and water can _____

_____.

4. **(formation)** It can take many years _____

_____.

5. **(visible)** The large city building _____

_____.

6. **(particles)** The air is filled with _____

_____.

7. **(structure)** A well-built stone wall is _____

_____.

8. **(contact)** The careless driver _____

_____.

Name _____

Read the selection. Complete the main idea and key details graphic organizer.

Main Idea
Detail
Detail
Detail

Name _____

Read the passage. Use the ask and answer questions strategy to help you understand what you read.

Migration

You may know people who have moved from one city to another. When
13 | people move, they usually stay in their new place for quite a while. Did
27 | you know that there are many animals that move two times a year? This
41 | regular movement is called migration.
46 | A migration is usually a round trip made between two areas. Most
58 | animals that migrate move when the seasons change in spring and fall.
70 | They go where there is better weather and more food. Some animals
82 | migrate to areas where their young will have a better chance to live.
95 | There are different types of migration. Many kinds of birds migrate
106 | between north and south. They live in northern areas in the spring and
119 | summer. In fall, when the weather turns cold, they fly south. In spring
132 | when the weather warms up, they fly north again.
141 | Other animals move between a higher place and a lower one when the
154 | seasons change. In summer, they make their homes high up on a mountain.
167 | When winter comes, they head to warmer areas down the slopes. Birds
179 | called mountain quail migrate in this way. These quail are birds that do not
193 | normally fly. In the fall, they walk down the mountain and in the spring
207 | they walk back up again!
212 | Some mammals and tropical birds live in climates that are very wet for
225 | at least part of the year. When the dry season comes, these animals move
239 | to a place that is wet during this season. When the rainy season returns,
253 | they go back home.
257 | How do these animals know when to migrate? Scientists who have
268 | studied this behavior think that animals know when seasons are about
279 | to change. They also seem to know where they are going and how to
293 | get there.

Name _____

Many animals migrate to and from the same places year after year. How do they know where to go? Many birds travel the same paths every year. These routes are called flyways. How do they know which path to follow? Human explorers have studied astronomy, and have used the sun, moon, and stars to guide them. Birds and other animals also use the stars and the sun to help them find their way. Some even use geographic features, such as rivers and mountain ranges, as landmarks. Biologists say some animals also seem to have the help of a built-in sense of direction.

Many types of birds, such as Canada geese, migrate each year.

Arctic terns are sea birds that fly huge distances. They can fly 22,000 miles in a year. That's farther than any other bird. Many terns live part of the year on the East Coast of North America and on islands in the Arctic Ocean. That is where they have their young. In late August, the terns begin their journey to Antarctica. They return to North America around the middle of June.

The monarch butterfly migrates up to 2,000 miles. They leave each fall to go to a warmer climate. In the fall, monarchs from Canada and the northeastern United States fly to a warmer climate in the mountains of central Mexico. Some from western North America seek warmer weather on the California coast.

Some fish migrate to reproduce. Salmon are known for making a hard journey to lay their eggs. Most salmon live in the ocean, but they are born in freshwater lakes and streams. To have their young, salmon travel back to the lakes and streams where they were born.

People have studied how animals migrate for hundreds of years. One famous migration is that of the swallows of Mission San Juan Capistrano in California. A popular song celebrated their annual return. Many of the swallows have now abandoned the Mission for other places in the area. But they haven't stopped migrating.

Name _____

A. Reread the passage and answer the questions.

1. What are two key details in the third paragraph?

_____

_____

_____

2. How are these details connected?

_____

_____

_____

3. What is the main idea in the third paragraph?

_____

_____

_____

B. Work with a partner. Read the passage aloud. Pay attention to rate and accuracy. Stop after one minute. Fill out the chart.

	Words Read	–	Number of Errors	=	Words Correct Score
First Read		–		=	
Second Read		–		=	

Name _____

Clues from Magnetic Rocks

Most rocks contain iron particles. When rocks are forming, their iron particles can align with Earth's magnetic field. The iron particles stay locked in this alignment. Scientists know that Earth's magnetic field has changed from north to south throughout time. This means that rocks formed at different times have different alignments of iron particles. Scientists can study the direction of iron particles in a rock sample to determine the age of the rock.

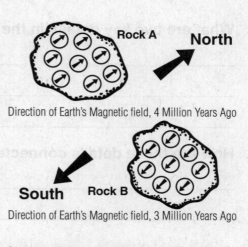

Rock A

North

Direction of Earth's Magnetic field, 4 Million Years Ago

South　Rock B

Direction of Earth's Magnetic field, 3 Million Years Ago

Iron particles in rocks can align with Earth's magnetic field direction.

Answer the questions about the text.

1. **How do you know this is expository text?**

   _____

   _____

2. **What three text features does this text include?**

   _____

   _____

3. **What is one fact that provides evidence to support the scientific concept?**

   _____

   _____

4. **How does the diagram help you understand the text?**

   _____

   _____

   _____

Name _____

Read each passage below. Use the Greek roots in the box and sentence clues to help you figure out the meaning of each word in bold. Write the word's meaning on the line. Then write your own sentence that uses the word in the same way.

Words	Greek Root/Meaning
tropical	*tropikos:* "turning, as toward the sun"
biology	*bio*: "life" + *logy*: "study"
astronomy	*astro*: "star" + *nomos*: "law"
arctic	*arktikos*: "of the north"

1. Some mammals and **tropical** birds live in climates that are very wet for at least part of the year.

   _____

   _____

2. Human explorers have studied **astronomy**, and have used the sun, moon, and stars to guide them.

   _____

   _____

3. **Biologists** say some animals also seem to have the help of a built-in sense of direction.

   _____

   _____

4. **Arctic** terns are sea birds that fly huge distances. Many terns live part of the year on the East Coast of North America and on islands in the Arctic Ocean.

   _____

   _____

Name _____

A. Read each word below. Write the word on the line and draw a slanted line (/) between the syllables. Then underline the vowel team.

1. grownup   _____

2. faucet   _____

3. footprint   _____

4. although   _____

5. moisture   _____

6. laughter   _____

7. grouchy   _____

8. entertain   _____

B. Read each sentence and circle the word that has a vowel team syllable. Underline the letters that form the vowel team.

9. Use caution when walking on wet or slippery surfaces.

10. I had a scary encounter with a spider in the garden.

11. She visited a small coastal city on her vacation.

12. They sat in the bleachers to watch the baseball game.

Name _____

Evidence is details and examples from a text that support a writer's ideas. The student who wrote the paragraph below cited evidence that shows how the author uses key details to support the main idea.

Topic sentence →   In "Migration" the author provides key details to support the main idea that many animals migrate. The author gives key details by providing examples of animals that migrate. Three of these examples are quails, Arctic terns, and monarch butterflies. Quails move up and down mountains. Terns move from North America to Antarctica in August and return in June. Monarch butterflies fly from Canada to Mexico in the fall. The author's use of these details supports the main idea that many animals migrate.

Evidence →

Concluding statement →

Write a paragraph about the text you have chosen. Cite evidence from the text to show how the author uses key details to support a main idea.

Write a topic sentence: _____

_____

Cite evidence from the text: _____

_____

_____

_____

_____

End with a concluding statement: _____

_____

Name _____

A. Read the draft model. Use the questions that follow the draft to help you think about what information could be replaced and what facts, details, or examples you could add to support the main idea.

Draft Model

A magnifying lens is useful because it makes small objects look larger. We used one today. Ms. Michaels likes them.

---

1. Which sentence above does not support the main idea and could be replaced?

2. What are some concrete examples of instances when a magnifying lens is useful?

3. What other relevant evidence in the form of facts, details, or quotations could be added to support the main idea?

B. Now revise the draft by replacing information that does not support the main idea and adding facts, examples, and other details that do.

_____

_____

_____

_____

_____

_____

_____

Name _____

| function | flexible | obstacle | artificial |
| techniques | mimic | collaborate | dedicated |

Use each pair of vocabulary words in a single sentence.

1. artificial, mimic

_____

_____

2. function, flexible

_____

_____

3. dedicated, obstacle

_____

_____

4. collaborate, techniques

_____

_____

Name _____

Read the selection. Complete the main idea and key details graphic organizer.

Main Idea
Detail
Detail
Detail

Name _____

Read the passage. Use the ask and answer questions strategy to check your understanding of new information or difficult facts.

Building a Green Town

12	On May 4, 2007, a tornado demolished the town of Greensburg, Kansas.
24	Nearly all the townspeople survived, but 95 percent of the town's buildings
35	were destroyed. With their town gone, the residents of Greensburg might have given up and moved away. Instead, they chose to stay and rebuild.
48	Within days of the storm, the people of Greensburg chose not only to
61	rebuild their town but to remake it. They resolved to reinvent their town so
75	that it lived up to its name. They would make Greensburg a green town.
89	**What Does It Mean to Be Green?**
96	Being green means being environmentally friendly. A person can
105	be green by recycling or composting. A person can use energy-saving
116	lightbulbs or public transportation. For a town, being green is more
127	complicated. It means using efficient and renewable power sources. It
137	means constructing buildings without harming the environment. It means
146	making sure the buildings use energy efficiently. It means gathering and
157	recycling everything from newspapers to rain water. It means making the
168	town walkable to reduce the use of cars and buses.
178	Greensburg residents knew what they wanted to do, but they did not
190	know how to do it. So they built a team. They brought in experts to guide
206	and teach them. Together, the residents and the experts set goals for
218	the new Greensburg and made a plan to reach those goals. They found
231	private companies and government agencies to help them pay for the
242	reconstruction. The greening of Greensburg began.

Name _____

The Greening of Greensburg

The first step in rebuilding the town was to clean up the wreckage from the storm. Reducing waste is an important part of being green. The townspeople did not want simply to throw away the broken pieces of their old town. They saved and reused as much as they could. Fallen trees were used to make furniture. Bricks were collected and used to build city hall. Cabinets, farm tools, and metal were also reused.

A tornado similar to the one shown above forced the town of Greensburg to rebuild.

Next, the residents of Greensburg made a remarkable commitment: to use "100 percent renewable energy, 100 percent of the time." This meant generating enough power for the whole town using natural resources such as the sun and wind year-round. To accomplish this, homes and public buildings were given geothermal heat pumps and solar panels. Geothermal pumps use heat from inside the earth. Solar panels turn sunlight into electricity or heat. The town partnered with an energy company to build a wind farm a few miles outside of town. Today, the wind farm provides more energy than the town uses. The "extra" energy is shared with other towns in Kansas.

In addition to using renewable energy, the town of Greensburg vowed to consume less energy overall. The new city buildings use 42 percent less energy than they had before the tornado. Greensburg's new homes use 40 percent less energy. The new streetlights use special lamps that are 40 percent more efficient than the old ones.

The efforts of Greensburg's residents worked. Their town is now a model sustainable community. It offers tours and information for people who want their towns to be more environmentally friendly. Greensburg is, as its citizens claim, "stronger, better, greener."

Name _____

A. Reread the passage and answer the questions.

1. **What are two key details in the first paragraph?**

_____

_____

_____

2. **How are these details connected to the rest of the text?**

_____

_____

_____

3. **What is the main idea of the third paragraph?**

_____

_____

_____

B. Work with a partner. Read the passage aloud. Pay attention to rate. Stop after one minute. Fill out the chart.

	Words Read	–	Number of Errors	=	Words Correct Score
First Read		–		=	
Second Read		–		=	

Name _____

Surf's Up!

Surfer Glen Hening saw how people worked together during the 1984 Summer Olympics. He decided to bring people together to help clean up California's coastal waters. Hening helped start the Surfrider Foundation to provide the best surfing experience for its members. The group helped people form local chapters and clubs to work on projects in their areas. Hundreds of these groups now collaborate with others around the country and the world to protect the ocean.

Purestock/Superstock

Surfrider local chapters have tested water quality at beaches.

Answer the questions about the text.

1. **How can you tell that this is expository text?**

   _____

   _____

2. **What is the main idea of the text?**

   _____

   _____

3. **What details in the first three sentences support the overall main idea of the text?**

   _____

   _____

4. **What kind of additional detail does the photo caption provide?**

   _____

   _____

Name _____

> *portare*: to carry   *moliri*: to build   *sumere*: to take
>
> *donare*: to present or give   *sol*: sun   *habitare*: to live or dwell

Use the Latin roots in the box above to identify the root in the underlined word below. Write the root on the line. Use context clues to determine the meaning of the word. Then write your own sentence using the word correctly.

1. On May 4, 2007, a tornado <u>demolished</u> the town of Greensburg, Kansas.

_____

_____

2. The <u>inhabitants</u> of Greensburg might have moved away.

_____

_____

3. A person can use energy-saving lightbulbs or public <u>transportation</u>.

_____

_____

4. <u>Solar</u> panels turn sunlight into electricity or heat.

_____

_____

5. The town of Greensburg vowed to <u>consume</u> less energy overall.

_____

_____

6. The residents of the town <u>donated</u> their time to help rebuild.

_____

_____

Name _____

A. Read each word below. Use a slanted line (/) to divide the word into syllables.

1. sample

2. cripple

3. tumble

4. gentle

5. purple

B. Read the following sentences. Underline each word that has a consonant + *le* syllable. Write the words on the lines and circle the letters that form the consonant + *le* syllable.

6. The rancher carried the saddle into the stable. _____ _____

7. She placed the steaming kettle on the table. _____ _____

8. Did the noble soldiers assemble at the armory? _____ _____

9. The terrible storm caused the cattle stampede. _____ _____

10. We saw an eagle, an otter, a beetle, and a snail. _____ _____

Name _____

> *Evidence* is details and examples from a text that support a writer's ideas. The student who wrote the paragraph below cited evidence that shows how the author uses key details to support a main idea.
>
> **Topic sentence** ⟶   In "Building a Green Town," the author provides key details to support the main idea that the residents of Greensburg did a good job of making their town environmentally friendly. The author gives key details by
>
> **Evidence** ⟶ providing examples of what the residents did to change their town. They reused old materials. They used sun and wind as energy sources. They put up new streetlights that save
>
> **Concluding statement** ⟶ energy. All of these details support the author's main idea that residents made Greensburg environmentally friendly.

Write a paragraph about the text you have chosen. Cite evidence from the text to show how the author uses key details to support a main idea.

Write a topic sentence: _____

_____

Cite evidence from the text: _____

_____

_____

_____

_____

End with a concluding statement: _____

_____

Name _____

A. Read the draft model. Use the questions that follow the draft to help you think about how you can strengthen the conclusion.

Draft Model

So that's what I found out about walking and running. They are both pretty interesting.

---

1. Where and how could the main idea be restated to help the reader remember information?

2. What key points could be summarized?

3. What interesting final thought could be added to give the reader more to think about?

B. Now revise the draft by adding and rearranging details to strengthen the conclusion.

_____

_____

_____

_____

_____

_____

_____

_____

_____

_____

_____

_____

Name _____

archaeologist   era   fragments   historian

intact   preserved   reconstruct   remnants

Finish each sentence using the vocabulary word provided.

1. **(historian)** If you like learning about the past, _____
_____ .

2. **(intact)** Some of the pottery was broken, but other pieces _____
_____ .

3. **(preserved)** The mummy discovered in the pyramid _____
_____ .

4. **(era)** The clothes we found were _____
_____ .

5. **(fragments)** We hoped to find a few _____
_____ .

6. **(reconstruct)** The group worked many hours _____
_____ .

7. **(remnants)** In the huge box of fabric scraps, _____
_____ .

8. **(archaeologist)** The ancient statue was _____
_____ .

Name _____

Read the selection. Complete the author's point of view graphic organizer.

Details	Author's Point of View
	→

Name _____

Read the two articles. Use the summarizing strategy to help you understand
each author's point of view.

WHAT WAS THE PURPOSE OF
THE NAZCA LINES?

Ancient Images

2	*The Nazca Lines are related to objects in the sky.*
12	The Nazca Lines are huge drawings found in the desert of southern Peru.
25	The Nazca people and earlier groups made the images 2,000 years ago
37	by removing dark gravel to show the light sand underneath. Some of the
50	drawings are shapes, like long lines or spirals. Other drawings are of animals
63	or plants. The drawings range in size from 150 feet to 950 feet. They are best
79	seen from a high altitude, such as from an airplane flying overhead.
91	The Answer Is in the Stars
97	Some people think that the Nazca Lines are related to astronomy.
108	Astronomy is the study of objects in the sky, such as planets or stars. One
123	twentieth-century scientist stated that some of the animal drawings looked
133	like constellations. She thought that the Nazca people drew patterns of
144	stars in the sky.
148	A Calendar for All Seasons
153	Another scientist agreed that the lines were related to the stars. He
165	believed the lines were a giant calendar. He noticed that the sun set over one
180	group of lines on the first day of winter each year. Noticing that sunrise and
195	sunset lined up with different lines during the year, he decided that the Nazca
209	used the lines to keep track of the months and seasons. By following the
223	movements of the sun and stars, they knew when to plant and harvest crops.
237	Research shows that there is a connection between the stars and
248	the Nazca Lines. Some of the Nazca sand patterns look like certain
260	constellations and the lines serve as a calendar when the sun lines up with
274	different drawings during the year. Scientists may not know exactly what
285	the Nazca used these lines for, but some are certain it relates to the stars.

Name _____

Ritual Paths

The Nazca Lines were used as ceremonial paths.

There is good reason to believe that the Nazca Lines had spiritual meaning for the Nazca people. They were a people of deep religious and cultural beliefs. We know of their beliefs from ancient artwork found on pottery and cloth. Many scientists think that the Nazca Lines were made for ceremonies related to the belief system of the Nazca. Since the desert land was so dry, these ceremonies were probably related to water.

Water was very important to the Nazca. The arid, or dry, desert land was not good for growing food. Without water, their crops would die. The people needed water to survive. They might have performed spiritual ceremonies to appeal for water.

Nazca Lines Spider

Ceremonial Paths Formed Images

Up close, the Nazca Lines look like dusty trails. Anthropologists who study the history and culture of the Nazca people think that's exactly what they are. Most of the drawings are formed of one single line or path. The Nazca could follow the paths to ceremonial locations.

Nazca Lines Monkey

Some researchers think the Nazca Lines were paths to ceremonial locations.

The Gift of Water

Archaeologists have studied fossils near the Nazca Lines. They have discovered piles of rocks at the ends of some of the lines. They think the piles were altars. People could leave ceremonial gifts there. The archaeologists have found seashell fossils near the altars. They think that the shells were used in rituals, or ceremonies. The Nazca believed that if their ceremonies were successful, they would get more water. Unfortunately, the Nazca ceremonies did not bring water. Eventually the Nazca people died out.

Religion and water were both important in Nazca culture. The Nazca people took part in water-related rituals. Remains of these rituals have been found near some Nazca Lines. This tells us that the Nazca Lines had a ceremonial purpose.

Name _____

A. Reread the passages and answer the questions.

1. What is the first author's position, or point of view, about the Nazca Lines?

_____

2. What facts from the text support this point of view?

_____

_____

3. What is the second author's position, or point of view, about the Nazca Lines?

_____

4. What facts from the text support this point of view?

_____

_____

B. Work with a partner. Read the passage aloud. Pay attention to expression and phrasing. Stop after one minute. Fill out the chart.

	Words Read	–	Number of Errors	=	Words Correct Score
First Read		–		=	
Second Read		–		=	

Name _____

Stonehenge Construction

Scientists have studied Stonehenge in England and can tell that builders from long ago had many skills. About 3000 B.C. construction began with the henge, a ditch and bank around the stones. Years later, wood pillars and stone blocks were added. Some bluestone blocks were used. Scientists proved that the bluestone came from Wales, 150 miles away. Many of the stones weigh over 45 tons and are over 24 feet tall. These facts show that the builders were very advanced.

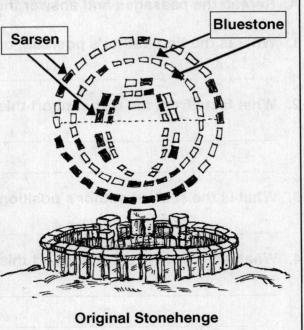

Original Stonehenge

Answer the questions about the text and diagram.

1. What is the author's point of view about the people who built Stonehenge?

   _____

   _____

2. How do you know the author is trying to persuade you to accept this point of view?

   _____

   _____

3. Why do you think the author included the diagram?

   _____

   _____

Name _____

Read each sentence. Underline the context clues in the sentence that help you define each word in bold. Then, in your own words, write the definition of the word in bold.

1. They are best seen from a high **altitude**, such as from an airplane flying overhead.

_____

2. One twentieth-century scientist stated that some of the animal drawings looked like **constellations**. She thought that the Nazca people drew patterns of stars in the sky.

_____

3. By following the movements of the sun and stars, they knew when to plant and **harvest** crops.

_____

4. **Archaeologists** have studied fossils near the Nazca Lines.

_____

5. They think the piles of rocks were **altars**. People could leave ceremonial gifts there.

_____

Name _____

A. Sort the words in the box below by their *r*-controlled vowel syllable. Write the words that have the same final syllable in the correct column.

pillar	crater	binocular
actor	equator	shatter

-ter	*-tor*	*-lar*
_____	_____	_____
_____	_____	_____

B. Read each sentence and underline the word with an *r*-controlled vowel syllable. Then write the word on the line and circle the *r*-controlled vowel syllable.

1. His dad is a commander in the navy. _____

2. What do you think caused the crater in the field? _____

3. You can find the scissors on the top shelf. _____

4. This cold makes my head feel terrible. _____

Name _____

Evidence is details and examples from a text that support a writer's opinion. The student who wrote the paragraph below cited evidence to show how well an author supports his or her position on a topic.

Topic sentence →   I think that the author of "Ancient Images" does a good job of supporting his or her position. In "Ancient Images," the author includes many facts to support the point that Nazca Lines are related to objects in the sky. The author includes the fact that two scientists agree that the Nazca lines are related to the stars. The author also presents the facts that Nazca sand patterns look like constellations and the sun lines up with different drawings during the year. I think these facts are good support of the author's position that Nazca lines are related to objects in the sky.

Evidence →

Concluding statement →

Write a paragraph about the text you have chosen. Cite evidence from the text to show how well an author supports his or her position.

Write a topic sentence: _____

_____

Cite evidence from the text: _____

_____

_____

_____

_____

End with a concluding statement: _____

_____

Name _____

A. Read the draft model. Use the questions that follow the draft to help you think about strong transitions you can add.

Draft Model

Millions of sports fans in the United States love football. People in other countries think football is slow and boring. They prefer the fast-moving game of soccer.

---

1. The jump from the first sentence to the second sentence is awkward. What transition can you add to the second sentence to show a connection between the sentences?

2. What other transitions could be added to improve the flow of the draft?

3. What transitions could be added to show the relationships between ideas?

B. Now revise the draft by adding transitions.

_____

_____

_____

_____

_____

_____

_____

Name _____

deeds	impress	wring	posed
sauntered	commenced	exaggeration	heroic

Write a complete sentence to answer each question below. In your answer, use the vocabulary word in bold.

1. Why do you think saving a child from a fire is a **heroic** act?

   _____

   _____

2. Why might a person try to **impress** someone with his or her singing?

   _____

   _____

3. What can happen if you do not **wring** out a mop? _____

   _____

4. If someone **sauntered** through a park, what would he or she be doing?

   _____

   _____

5. Why might a person make an **exaggeration** about something?

   _____

   _____

6. What are two good **deeds** that you have seen people do?

   _____

   _____

7. What is something that you have **posed** for recently? _____

   _____

8. How does a referee signal that a game has **commenced**? _____

   _____

Name _____

Read the selection. Complete the point of view graphic organizer.

Details	Point of View

Name _____

Read the passage. Use the visualizing strategy to help you picture what you are reading.

Pecos Bill's Wild Ride

	Pecos Bill was a cowboy. Perhaps it would be better to say that Pecos
14	Bill was *the* cowboy. No one threw a rope faster or rode a bronco longer
29	than Bill. He could lasso a steer and have it ready to brand before the lariat
45	was off his saddle horn. Once, he got on a wild horse at dawn and was still
62	riding when the tame beast finally bedded down for the night. Of course,
75	that was a week later. Bill himself would be glad to tell you that he was
91	the original cowboy and that the others were just copies—and he'd be
104	saying it in all modesty!
109	There was one time Pecos Bill got thrown. Of course, no cowhand likes
122	to confess to being tossed off his mount. Still, even Bill would likely admit
136	to this particular tumble. He might even tell the tale with pride.
148	It happened on the day Pecos Bill invented the rodeo. Bill was riding
161	the trail with a group of cowherds. They were telling stories about their
174	wild rides. To Bill, their accounts had the taste of whoppers about them.
187	He wasn't about to accuse anyone of telling lies, though, so he kept this
201	feeling to himself.
204	It was just then that the weather changed. The wind picked up, and the
218	sky took on an unusual shade of yellow. Turning in his saddle, Bill saw a
233	big, black twister bearing down on the herd. He could hear an odd sound
247	like a cross between a freight train and a bear's growl. The noise got
261	louder as the storm approached. "I reckon there's a tornado coming our
273	way," he remarked. "You boys round up the herd. If you all don't mind,
287	I'm going to take a little ride of my own. Don't wait up."
300	With that, Bill headed back down the trail toward the roaring storm.
312	While he rode, he took his lasso off the saddle horn and began spinning it
327	above his head.

Name _____

As the lasso spun, Bill played out a little more rope and then a little more again. When the loop was about as big as a Texas watermelon, he gave his wrist a snap. The lasso sailed up till it was about level with a mountaintop. Bill gave his wrist another flick, and the noose dropped down neatly over the neck of the twister.

With a shout, Bill made a mighty leap and landed squarely on the tornado's back. Right away, that whirlwind started rearing and bucking. It lost interest in the herd of cattle on the trail and took off in a northwesterly direction at a gallop. In its mad dash, it pulled up trees, mowed down prairie grasses, and cut a trench across the dry flatlands. Later, water started flowing down that trench, and people took to calling it the Pecos River in honor of Bill's ride.

All the while, Bill kept his seat. He pressed his knees into the sides of his stormy steed, gripped the rope in one hand, and held on to his hat with the other. The pair left Texas, crossed New Mexico, and entered Arizona. As they went, the storm bucked and roared. Bill just hung on and whispered to it, trying to gentle it. Despite the sweet nothings he murmured, it would not be tamed.

They were almost in Nevada when Bill sensed the storm was losing energy and relaxed some. That's when the tornado acted. It spun so hard that its tail cut a broad, deep canyon in the rocks. (Today, folks call that the Grand Canyon.) Finally, with its last bit of strength, the storm threw Pecos Bill. He tumbled head over heels, flew over the Mojave, and landed in California with a mighty wallop. When he'd caught his breath, he saw he'd hit the ground so hard, there was a crater in it. "If anyone else took a fall like that," he said to himself, "they might have died." (That's probably why nowadays people call his landing place Death Valley.)

And that's how Pecos Bill created the rodeo.

Name _____

A. Reread the passage and answer the questions.

1. Is the narrator of the text a character in the story or someone outside the story? How can you tell?

_____

_____

2. How does the reader know what the narrator thinks about Pecos Bill?

_____

3. What point of view does the author use in the text and how do you know?

_____

_____

_____

B. Work with a partner. Read the passage aloud. Pay attention to expression. Stop after one minute. Fill out the chart.

	Words Read	–	Number of Errors	=	Words Correct Score
First Read		–		=	
Second Read		–		=	

Name _____

Stormie and the Octopus

Old Stormalong was sailing over the deepest part of the ocean when the anchor was knocked loose and dropped to the bottom of the ocean. It caught on something and yanked the ship to a stop. Stormie the Brave dove in to untangle the anchor. Soon Stormie popped up and told his men to haul in the anchor. "An old octopus was holding the anchor, and I had to arm wrestle him for it," he said. "Then I tied all his arms and legs in knots."

Answer the questions about the text.

1. **How do you know this text is a tall tale?**

   _____

   _____

2. **Write two examples of hyberbole that are found in the text. How is each example humorous?**

   _____

   _____

3. **What challenge did Stormie the Brave face, and how was he a hero?**

   _____

   _____

Name _____

A. Underline the word in each passage that is the synonym or antonym for the word in bold.

1. (antonym) Bill himself would be glad to tell you that he was the **original** cowboy and that the others were just copies.

2. (synonym) There was one time Pecos Bill got **thrown**. Of course, no cowhand likes to confess to being tossed off his mount.

3. (synonym) To Bill, their accounts had the taste of **whoppers** about them. He wasn't about to accuse anyone of telling lies, though.

4. (synonym) All the while, Bill kept his seat. He pressed his knees into the sides of his stormy steed, **gripped** the rope in one hand, and held on to his hat with the other.

5. (antonym) As they went, the storm bucked and **roared**. Bill just hung on and whispered to it.

B. Circle the word in each line that is an antonym for the word in bold.

1. **confess**   speak   admit   deny

2. **flatland**   mountain   prairie   plain

3. **murmured**   whispered   shouted   hugged

Name _____

A. Read the words in each row. Underline the word that has the final /əl/ sound. Then write the letters that make the final /əl/ sound in each word you underlined.

1. practical   winner   _____

2. prevail   bushel   _____

3. chuckle   surprise   _____

4. nozzle   human   _____

5. hungry   pretzel   _____

6. fable   chicken   _____

B. Read the words in each row. Underline the word that has the final /ən/ sound. Then write the letters that make the final /ən/ sound in each word you underlined.

7. barrel   mountain   _____

8. tougher   heron   _____

9. lengthen   credit   _____

10. gushing   captain   _____

11. hasten   summer   _____

12. stranded   slogan   _____

Name _____

Evidence is details and examples from a text that support a writer's ideas. The student who wrote the paragraph below cited evidence that shows how the author uses exaggeration to develop the main character.

Topic sentence ⟶ In "Pecos Bill's Wild Ride," the author uses exaggeration to show that the main character, Pecos Bill, is very strong.

Evidence ⟶ The author uses exaggeration to describe Bill's actions when he lassos the tornado. Bill made the loop as big as a Texas watermelon. He threw it as high as a mountaintop. Later, when Bill is thrown off the tornado, he makes a crater in the ground but is not hurt. The author's use of these exaggerated details show that Pecos Bill is very strong.

Concluding statement ⟶

Write a paragraph about a tall tale you have chosen. Cite evidence from the text to show how an author uses exaggeration to develop the main character.

Write a topic sentence: _____

_____

Cite evidence from the text: _____

_____

_____

_____

_____

End with a concluding statement: _____

_____

Name _____

A. Read the draft model. Use the questions that follow the draft to help you think about how you can enhance the style and tone to suit the text's purpose.

Draft Model

Haley, a soccer player, collected used soccer jerseys and sent them to Guatemalan children. Her efforts helped create a global soccer team.

---

1. What details would help clarify the author's purpose for writing?

2. What details would make the text more engaging?

3. What details would convey the author's attitude toward Haley? How else can you strengthen the tone?

B. Now revise the draft by adding details to strengthen the text's style and tone.

_____

_____

_____

_____

_____

_____

_____

Name _____

perplexed	astounded	precise	inquisitive
suspicious	concealed	interpret	reconsider

Finish each sentence using the vocabulary word provided.

1. **(precise)** In order for a word's definition to be clear, _____

_____.

2. **(reconsider)** There was a sudden change in the weather, so _____

_____.

3. **(interpret)** We had a hard time understanding the play, so _____

_____.

4. **(perplexed)** The stranger asked for directions because _____

_____.

5. **(astounded)** We expected the acrobat's performance to be dull, but _____

_____.

6. **(inquisitive)** I didn't care about the mystery, but my sister _____

_____.

7. **(suspicious)** The salesperson didn't seem honest, which _____

_____.

8. **(concealed)** We wanted to eat our snacks right away, but _____

_____.

Name _____

Read the selection. Complete the point of view graphic organizer.

Details	Point of View

Name _____

Read the passage. Use the strategy of visualizing to check your understanding.

A Penny Saved

	SETTING: A family living room in the evening. MOM and DAD sit
12	together on a couch while children REX and MANDY sit cross-legged on
24	the floor in front of them. TAD stands facing them with graphs and charts
38	posted on an easel behind him. A bright pink piggy bank sits on a small
53	table in the center of the stage.
60	TAD: You're all probably perplexed as to why I've called this
71	emergency family meeting. It is because of this! [points to the piggy
83	bank] It seems that someone, perhaps one of you, has been raiding our
96	vacation fund!
98	MOM [hiding a smile]: And what evidence, may I ask, has led you to be
113	so suspicious?
115	TAD: Well, we all know that a penny saved is a penny earned, and
129	we've stashed away lots of spare change over the months. We were
141	planning on using that money for our summer adventure. But lately I've
153	observed that our piggy bank has been losing weight.
162	REX: It doesn't look any thinner to me.
170	TAD: Well, if you look at this chart and spreadsheet [turns to point at
184	easel behind him], you'll see a steady decline in the bank's weight over the
198	past weeks.
200	MOM [to DAD]: Did you help him make those on your computer?
212	DAD [to MOM]: He likes numbers and charts as much as I do. The
226	acorn doesn't fall far from the tree.
233	MANDY: So you think that one of us has been stealing money?
245	TAD: That is a precise summary of my investigation.
254	MOM: Well, knowing what a great detective you are, I'm sure you left
267	no stone unturned. What other evidence do you have?

Name _____

TAD: As you all know, a previous incident [looks at REX] resulted in our placing a strip of security tape here across the bank's stopper. I cleverly marked the tape one day. On the very next day, I found that the tape had been replaced!

MANDY: Rex, how did you know where Mom keeps the tape?

REX: Why are you blaming me? I didn't do it.

The family's piggy bank was mysteriously losing weight.

MOM: Hold on a moment, Mandy. You should look before you leap. We need to consider Tad's evidence first.

DAD: I'm sure there's a reasonable explanation.

MOM [stands up]: There is another explanation. After all, there are two sides to every coin. Tad, as it turns out, I guess I'm your so-called "thief."

TAD [astounded]: You? Why would you take money from the piggy bank? You and Dad have lots of money already!

MOM: Well, it may seem as though we're rich to you, but sometimes we don't have as much money on hand as we need. And it's not as if I "stole" anything. Let me ask you this: Every morning on your way to school, what do I give you kids?

REX [proudly]: Three quarters each for snacks!

MOM: Tad, pick up the piggy bank and give it a shake. [He does.] Tell me what you hear.

TAD: Not as much change as two days ago, that's for sure. [shaking again] Maybe some rustling sounds, like paper.

MOM: Like dollar bills, perhaps? I've been taking out coins and replacing them with bills whenever I needed spare change for your snacks. That's why the bank has been getting lighter.

TAD: Well, I guess all's well that ends well, then.

MOM: Tad, they say that a fool and his money are soon parted. With that in mind, a smart boy like you will never go broke!

Name _____

A. Reread the passage and answer the questions.

1. Which speaker calls the family meeting, and why?

_____

_____

2. From Tad's point of view, what evidence does he have that shows someone has been stealing?

_____

_____

3. Whom might Tad suspect, and how do you know?

_____

_____

4. Which speaker offers a different point of view about what caused the piggy bank's weight loss? What is that point of view?

_____

_____

B. Work with a partner. Read the passage aloud. Pay attention to rate and accuracy. Stop after one minute. Fill out the chart.

	Words Read	–	Number of Errors	=	Words Correct Score
First Read		–		=	
Second Read		–		=	

Name _____

A Surprise in the Attic

Scene One

(Setting: A family's attic. RON and JOHN, 10-year-old twins,
are ransacking boxes.)

RON: We'll never get our historical costumes done on time!

JOHN: With all of this stuff here, we'll figure something out. Right?

RON (finds a sheet of paper): Look! Someone concealed a telegram in this trunk. (He reads it.) It's dated April 10, 1912. It says, "I will not be there. I have missed Titanic's noon launch."

JOHN: An ancestor of ours missed the Titanic! I wonder who?

Answer the questions about the text.

1. **How can you tell that this text is from a play?**

   _____

2. **What do the stage directions tell you?**

   _____

   _____

3. **What mystery emerges at the end of the text?**

   _____

4. **What can you infer is the reason that the twins are searching the attic? Where did you find the clues?**

   _____

   _____

   _____

   _____

Name _____

Read each passage. Underline each adage or proverb. Then write its meaning on the lines.

1. TAD: Well, we all know that a penny saved is a penny earned, and we've stashed away lots of spare change over the months. We were planning on using that money for our summer adventure.

   _____

   _____

2. MOM: Hold on a moment, Mandy. You should look before you leap. We need to consider Tad's evidence first.

   _____

   _____

3. MOM [stands up]: There is another explanation. After all, there are two sides to every coin. Tad, as it turns out, I guess I'm your so-called "thief."

   _____

   _____

4. MOM: Tad, they say that a fool and his money are soon parted. With that in mind, a smart boy like you will never go broke!

   _____

   _____

Name _____

A. Read each word and circle the prefix. Then write a definition of the word based on the meaning of the prefix.

1. unimportant _____

2. reunite _____

3. misguide _____

4. nonspecific _____

5. dishonest _____

6. underwater _____

B. Add a prefix to each word in parentheses to make a new word. Then write the new word to complete each sentence.

7. **(usual)** Some people think it is _____ that she wears only pink clothes.

8. **(connect)** You must pull out the plug in order to _____ the television.

9. **(wrap)** The boy had to _____ the gift after the baby tore the paper off.

10. **(friendly)** She tried not to be _____ and greeted all the visitors with a smile.

Name _____

Evidence is details and examples from a text that support a writer's ideas. The student who wrote the paragraph below cited evidence that supports an opinion about characters in two mystery stories.

Topic sentence →   I think Alex in "Where's Brownie?" is a better problem-solver than Tad in "A Penny Saved." In "Where's Brownie?"

Evidence → Alex is good at noticing things. She notices Brownie is missing and the bag is wet. She also uses new information from Evan to find Brownie. Tad in "A Penny Saved" notices the piggy bank is lighter. He also makes a chart to help him. But Tad does not use new information to solve the mystery. Tad's mom tells him what

Concluding statement → happened. That's why I think Alex in "Where's Brownie?" is a better problem-solver than Tad.

Write a paragraph about the two mysteries you have chosen. Choose a character from each mystery to compare. Give your opinion as to which character is a better problem-solver. Cite evidence to support your opinion.

Write a topic sentence: _____

_____

Cite evidence from the text: _____

_____

_____

_____

_____

End with a concluding statement: _____

_____

Name _____

A. Read the draft model. Use the questions that follow the draft to help you think about what details you can add to develop the characters.

Draft Model

Rion told Zach to open it.

"I'm not touching it," responded Zach.

"Okay. I'll do it. Move over," said Rion.

---

1. What details can you add to make the characters more real? What details would help readers visualize the characters?

2. How can you adjust the dialogue to help it reveal what the characters are like?

3. What other details would help to show the characters' personalities? What details would show why they respond to each other as they do?

B. Now revise the draft by adding details to better develop the characters of Rion and Zach.

_____

_____

_____

_____

_____

_____

_____

Name _____

| anticipation | defy | entitled | neutral |
| outspoken | reserved | sought | unequal |

Use each pair of vocabulary words in a single sentence.

1. anticipation, reserved

_____

_____

2. defy, unequal

_____

_____

3. entitled, outspoken

_____

_____

4. neutral, sought

_____

_____

Name _____

Read the selection. Complete the author's point of view graphic organizer.

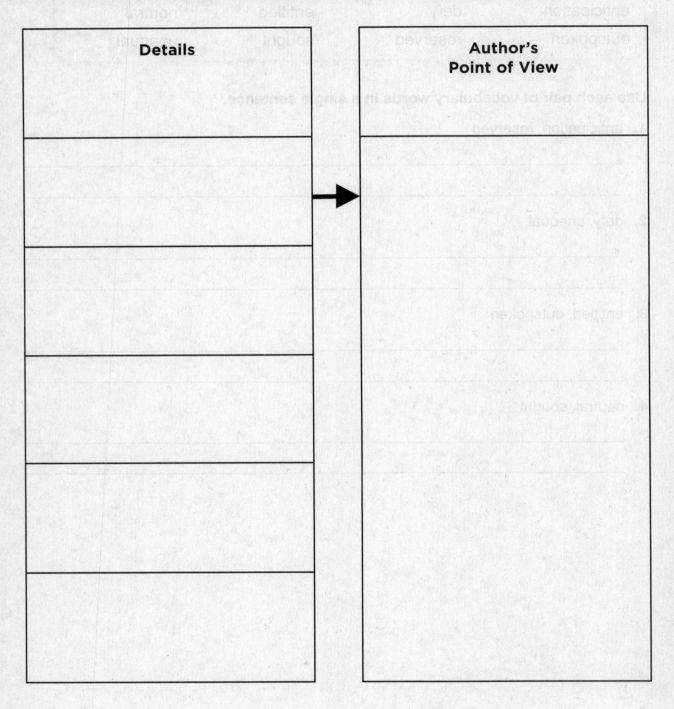

Details	Author's Point of View

Name _____

Read the passage. Use the summarize strategy to recognize and remember what you learned.

A Warrior for Women's Rights

	In January 1917, a group of women marched silently in front of the
13	White House. Each carried a banner asking for the right to vote. One
26	banner read, "Mr. President, how long must women wait for liberty?"
37	These women, called Silent Sentinels, picketed outside the White House
47	almost every day for eighteen months. Passersby attacked the women and
58	called them names, but the demonstrators continued their silent march.
68	These women were the first ever to protest in front of the White House.
82	Their leader was a brave young woman named Alice Paul.

	Becoming a Suffragette
92	
95	Alice Paul was born in 1885 in Moorestown, New Jersey. She came
107	from a Quaker family that believed in women's education and women's
118	equality, uncommon beliefs for the time. Her mother worked for women's
129	suffrage and brought young Alice to her suffrage meetings.
138	Paul graduated high school at the top of her class and went on to
152	college. She earned degrees in biology and sociology before going to
163	England to study social work.
168	Her stay in England transformed Paul. She met Emmeline and
178	Christabel Pankhurst, leaders of the women's suffrage movement in
187	England. They taught Paul a new way to fight for women's equality.
199	American suffragists had chosen quieter ways to push for women's
209	rights. They wrote letters, passed around petitions, and held private
219	meetings with political leaders. English suffragists believed in "deeds, not
229	words." They held parades. They formed picket lines. They went on hunger
241	strikes. Alice Paul returned to the United States with a fighting spirit.

Name _____

Taking to the Streets

Alice Paul had always been shy, but she was not afraid of confrontation. She learned in England that confrontation was the best way to bring attention to the issue of women's suffrage.

Her first act as a leader in the American suffrage movement was to organize a parade in Washington, D.C. She scheduled

Women protested in front of the White House for their right to vote.

the parade for the day before President Woodrow Wilson took office. On March 3, 1913, thousands of women marched down Pennsylvania Avenue carrying banners demanding the right to vote. The marchers were attacked, and the police did very little to help them. Despite the attacks, Paul got what she wanted: attention for her cause.

Four years later, when women still did not have the vote, Paul organized the Silent Sentinels. Again, the police did not protect the protestors. Instead, they arrested the women. Each day, a few more were arrested. At first, the women were released quickly. As their picketing continued, however, their jail sentences became longer.

In October 1917, Paul was arrested for organizing the protests. She and the other suffragists were mistreated in jail. Newspapers printed stories about the women's treatment. The stories earned public sympathy for the women.

President Wilson announced that he supported Paul's cause. In 1918, he sent Congress a constitutional amendment that would give women the right to vote. Two years later, the amendment—the 19th—became law.

A Tireless Crusader

Paul's efforts to achieve women's equality did not end with the passage of the 19th Amendment. In 1921, she wrote the Equal Rights Amendment, which sought to protect women against discrimination. She fought for its passage until her death in 1977.

Name _____

A. Reread the passage and answer the questions.

1. **What descriptions and details from the first two paragraphs help you determine the author's point of view?**

_____

_____

_____

2. **How do the headings throughout the passage connect to the author's point of view?**

_____

_____

_____

3. **After reading the entire passage, how would you summarize the author's point of view?**

_____

_____

_____

_____

B. Work with a partner. Read the passage aloud. Pay attention to phrasing. Stop after one minute. Fill out the chart.

	Words Read	–	Number of Errors	=	Words Correct Score
First Read		–		=	
Second Read		–		=	

Name _____

A Rolling Movement

When he was 14 years old, Ed Roberts became paralyzed from polio. In his twenties he sought admission to college but was told that his physical condition made it too problematic. Ed protested and gained acceptance. He started a group of physically challenged students on campus called "The Rolling Quads" to improve access to services and facilities. Throughout his life, Ed founded and supported similar groups around the world. For that reason he is known as the "father of the independent living movement."

In the United States there are laws and acts that protect the rights of all students.

Answer the questions about the text.

1. What kind of text is this? How do you know?

    _____

    _____

2. What text features does this text include?

    _____

    _____

3. How does the title relate to the text?

    _____

    _____

4. What additional information does the photo and its caption provide?

    _____

    _____

Name _____

Circle any prefixes or suffixes in the word in bold in each sentence. Then write the meaning of the word on the line.

1. Passersby attacked the women and called them names, but the **demonstrators** continued their silent march.

   Word meaning: _____

2. She came from a Quaker family that believed in women's education and women's equality, **uncommon** beliefs for the time.

   Word meaning: _____

3. She earned degrees in **biology** and sociology before going to England to study social work.

   Word meaning: _____

4. Her stay in England **transformed** Paul.

   Word meaning: _____

5. Alice Paul had always been shy, but she was not afraid of **confrontation**.

   Word meaning: _____

6. She and the other suffragists were **mistreated** in jail.

   Word meaning: _____

Name _____

A. Read each sentence. Circle the accented syllable in each underlined word. Use a dictionary to help you.

1. The new puppy seemed quite <u>content</u> on the blanket.

2. The paper <u>insert</u> slipped out of the magazine.

3. I hope they will not <u>desert</u> us here in the forest.

4. Why did the coach <u>subject</u> us to a tough practice?

5. We tried to <u>insert</u> the coins into the machine.

6. She went to the <u>desert</u> to photograph sand dunes.

B. Read each sentence. Write the part of speech of the underlined word.

7. There is no <u>excuse</u> for bad manners. _____

8. Will you please <u>excuse</u> me for a moment? _____

9. Dad was <u>present</u> for the student play. _____

10. Mom wrapped the <u>present</u> in newspaper. _____

11. They will <u>present</u> the award at noon. _____

12. Which <u>subject</u> in school is your favorite? _____

Name _____

Evidence is details and examples from a text that support a writer's ideas. The student who wrote the paragraph below cited evidence to explain how details in a biography show an author's point of view.

Topic sentence →   Many details in "A Warrior for Women's Rights" show that the author thinks Alice Paul was a great leader. The author describes Alice Paul as brave. She had a fighting spirit and was not afraid of confrontation. The author also describes the parades and protests Alice organized. Alice was arrested and mistreated in jail. But she still fought for women's equality until her death. All of these details show that the author thinks Alice Paul was a great leader.

Evidence →

Concluding statement →

Write a paragraph about the text you have chosen. Cite evidence from the text to explain how details show the author's point of view.

Write a topic sentence: _____

_____

Cite evidence from the text: _____

_____

_____

_____

_____

End with a concluding statement: _____

_____

Name _____

A. Read the draft model. Use the questions that follow the draft to help you think about logical order.

Draft Model

The students went to the park. They made sandwiches before they came.
They had learned about the many homeless people in the area. They saw it in the
newspaper that morning.

---

1. How could ideas be reordered to make the text easier to follow?

2. What time-order words could be added to clarify the order of events?

3. What other details could be added or changed to make the organization of the
   text more logical?

B. Now revise the draft by reordering ideas to make the organization more logical.

_____

_____

_____

_____

_____

_____

_____

_____

_____

_____

Name _____

| affect | cycle | absorb | glaciers |
| seeps | circulates | conserve | necessity |

Write a complete sentence to answer each question below. In your answer, use the vocabulary word in bold.

1. How can cold weather **affect** plants in a garden?

   _____

2. What kind of **cycle** might you learn about at school?

   _____

3. What can be used to **absorb** liquid that is spilled?

   _____

4. What kind of place would you need to visit in order to see **glaciers**?

   _____

5. What should you do when water **seeps** under the sink?

   _____

6. What is one way that air **circulates** through a house?

   _____

7. How can we **conserve** water at home?

   _____

8. What is a **necessity** for all human beings?

   _____

Name _____

Read the selection. Complete the author's point of view graphic organizer.

Details		Author's Point of View
	→	

Name _____

Read the passage. Use the summarize strategy to help you understand what you read.

The Wonders of Water

Water as a Natural Resource

5	Water is a natural resource that makes life on Earth possible. People,
17	animals, and plants cannot live without it. Yet, in many places in the
30	world, people are running low on water to meet their needs. More and
43	more people need larger amounts of water for drinking, energy, farming,
54	and industry. These growing needs influence, or affect, the demand for
65	available fresh water. Also, waste from farming, business, and energy
75	can pollute water in rivers, lakes, and the ocean. Such pollution reduces
87	available water supplies even more.
92	It may seem odd that some people are running low on water because
105	Earth's surface has more water than anything else. Seventy percent of
116	Earth's surface is ocean, and oceans hold about 97 percent of Earth's
128	water. However, ocean water is too salty to be usable. People need
140	fresh water. Fortunately, there is something that turns ocean water into
151	fresh water.

The Water Cycle

153	
156	Earth's water is always moving and changing in a circular pattern.
167	This repeating system is called the water cycle. The water cycle plays an
180	important role in providing people with fresh water as a natural resource.
192	The sun provides energy to the water cycle. As the sun heats ocean
205	water, some of the liquid evaporates; that is, it changes into a gas, or
219	vapor. Wind carries the vapor high into the air, where much of it cools and
234	forms clouds.

Name _____

Some of Earth's water may get stored outside the water cycle. This storage affects how much water is available as a resource. For example, when water freezes in cold weather, it stops taking part in the water cycle. As the weather warms up, the ice melts and returns as water to the cycle.

Water is stored for longer periods of time in large ice floes called glaciers and in polar ice. These kinds of ice are not affected much by the seasons. However, in recent decades they have been slowly melting and growing smaller.

Water Above Earth

As the water vapor in the air cools, it condenses; that is, it changes to liquid water, forming tiny drops. These water droplets join with bits of dust, salt, and smoke to form clouds. The wind helps hold clouds in the air and circulates, or moves, them from one place to another. When a cloud has more water than it can hold, water drops fall from the cloud. This water falls to Earth, where it may flow in streams and rivers back to the ocean, providing people with fresh water along the way.

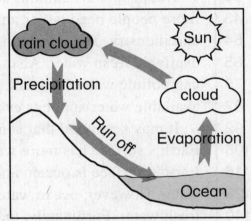

The water cycle provides water that people use as a resource.

Water In the Earth

Some of the water that falls to Earth is absorbed, or soaked up, by the ground. Some of this water will stay near the surface in the soil. This water may feed plants and trees. In turn, plants and trees give off water vapor from their leaves.

However, gravity pulls some of the water deeper below the surface where it fills spaces between rocks and sand. This forms bodies of water in the ground. Ground water may be stored in the Earth for a long time, or it may seep, or leak, into other bodies of water, such as rivers. In many places people drill wells down to the ground water and bring it to the surface for drinking or farming.

Name _____

A. Reread the passage and answer the questions.

1. In the first paragraph, the author describes a problem with Earth's water supply. What details give clues about the author's point of view?

_____

_____

_____

_____

2. Why does the author provide a detailed description of the water cycle?

_____

_____

3. Overall, would you describe the author's point of view in this passage as biased or balanced? Explain.

_____

_____

_____

B. Work with a partner. Read the passage aloud. Pay attention to accuracy and expression. Stop after one minute. Fill out the chart.

	Words Read	–	Number of Errors	=	Words Correct Score
First Read		–		=	
Second Read		–		=	

Name _____

Renewing the Future

For many years, temperatures in New Mexico have increased and rainfall has decreased. In Jemez Pueblo, sunshine is plentiful. This is a valuable natural resource for the Pueblo. The Jemez tribe is planning to tap this resource. They will build a solar energy plant on their lands. They will sell the energy they produce. The Pueblo will use the income from the plant to improve their drinking water system. Tribal leaders say this project will benefit future generations. Solar power will also help the environment by cutting down on the use of fossil fuels.

New Mexico August Temperatures

Dates	1900–1939	1940–1979	1980–2010
Range	68.5–74.4	68.8–73.5	69–76.5
Average	71.3	71.5	71.8

Answer the questions about the text.

1. How do you know this is expository text?

   _____

2. What does the heading tell you about the text?

   _____

   _____

3. What text feature does this text include? What information does it give you?

   _____

   _____

4. What do you learn from the text feature?

   _____

Name _____

Read each passage. Underline the context clues that help you figure out the meaning of each word in bold. Then write the word's meaning on the line.

1. More and more people need larger amounts of water for drinking, energy, farming, and industry. These growing needs **influence**, or affect, the demand for available fresh water.

   _____

2. Earth's water is always moving and changing in a circular pattern. This repeating system is called the water **cycle**.

   _____

3. The sun provides energy to the water cycle. As the sun heats ocean water, some of the liquid **evaporates**; that is, it changes into a gas, or vapor.

   _____

4. Water is stored for longer periods of time in large ice floes called **glaciers** and in polar ice. These kinds of ice are not affected much by the seasons.

   _____

5. However, gravity pulls some of the water deeper below the surface where it fills spaces between rocks and sand. This forms bodies of water in the ground. Ground water may be stored in the Earth for a long time, or it may **seep**, or leak, into other bodies of water, such as rivers.

   _____

Name _____

A. Read each word aloud. Write the word, divide the syllables with a slanted line (/), and underline the letters that make the /zhər/ or /chər/ sounds. Then write the letters that stand for the sounds.

1. mixture _____ _____

2. exposure _____ _____

3. feature _____ _____

4. moisture _____ _____

5. measure _____ _____

6. creature _____ _____

7. seizure _____ _____

8. pleasure _____ _____

B. Look at the syllables and sounds you identified above. Answer the questions.

1. How can the /zhər/ sound be spelled?

_____

2. How can the /chər/ sound be spelled?

_____

Name _____

Evidence is details and examples from a text that support a writer's ideas. The student who wrote the paragraph below cited evidence that shows how the author uses reasons and evidence to support a point.

Topic sentence →   In "The Wonders of Water," the author uses reasons and evidence to support the point that water is an important natural resource. The author states that people need fresh

Evidence → water. People need water for drinking, energy, farming, and industry. The water cycle provides people with fresh water. Ocean water evaporates, forms clouds, and falls down to the Earth as rain or snow. The water cycle brings people fresh

Concluding statement → water. These reasons and evidence support the author's point that water is an important natural resource.

Write a paragraph about the text you have chosen. Cite evidence from the text to show how the author uses reasons and evidence to support a point.

Write a topic sentence: _____

_____

Cite evidence from the text: _____

_____

_____

_____

_____

End with a concluding statement: _____

_____

Name _____

A. Read the draft model. Use the questions that follow the draft to help you think about how you can add transitions to connect ideas.

Draft Model

Water is necessary for life. Plants and animals need water to survive. People should conserve water.

---

1. What transitions can you add to help show the relationship between the ideas in the first and second sentences?

2. How does the idea in the last sentence relate to the other ideas? What transition could be added to express this relationship?

3. What other details can you add to help develop the ideas?

B. Now revise the draft by adding transition words to connect ideas.

_____

_____

_____

_____

_____

_____

_____

_____

_____

Name _____

plumes   meaningful   barren   expression

Finish each sentence using the vocabulary word provided.

1. **(plumes)** At the zoo our class _____
_____ .

2. **(barren)** The desert land was _____
_____ .

3. **(meaningful)** The old letter from her father was _____
_____ .

4. **(expression)** In his notebook _____
_____ .

Name _____

Read the selection. Complete the theme graphic organizer.

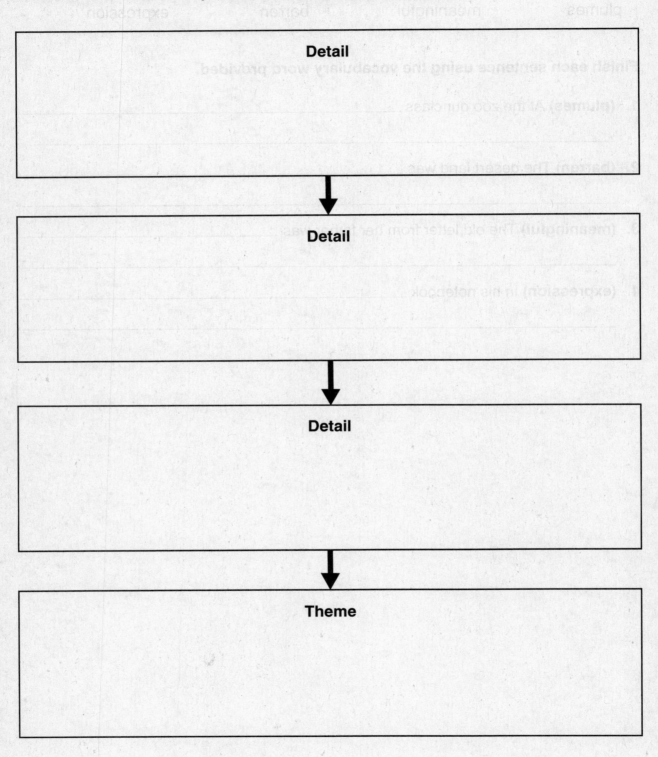

Detail

Detail

Detail

Theme

Name _____

Read the passage. As you read, check your understanding by asking yourself what theme or message the author wants to convey.

Grandpa's Shed

5	My grandpa is a mountain,
	Brooding, looming, tall.
8	I stand in his shadow, silent as a stone.
17	Rattling rusty paint cans,
21	He gestures toward the shed. I gape.
28	That shed's a squat gray mushroom,
34	Needing more than paint to fix.
40	The old man's hands are vises,
46	Prying open paint cans lightning fast.
52	Astonished, awed, I gasp aloud,
57	"Red, yellow, green—and PURPLE!"
62	My words explode like fireworks.
67	Anticipating anger,
69	my mouth shuts like a trap.
75	Grandpa merely dips his brush,
80	Paints a horse and hound.
85	"The horse I harnessed as a boy,
92	Dog was mine too."
96	Impulse strikes—a flash of fire.
102	I seize a brush,
106	Soon swishing, swirling pictures.
110	With each stroke, a story,
115	My words painting pictures.
119	We share that shed like one vast canvas,
127	His strokes to mine, my words to his.
135	We step back, gazing at stories told.

Name _____

A. Reread the passage and answer the questions.

1. What key details in the poem describe events that happened?

_____

_____

_____

2. What key details tell you about the speaker's feelings?

_____

_____

_____

3. What is the theme, or important message, of the poem?

_____

_____

B. Work with a partner. Read the passage aloud. Pay attention to expression and phrasing. Stop after one minute. Fill out the chart.

	Words Read	–	Number of Errors	=	Words Correct Score
First Read		–		=	
Second Read		–		=	

Name _____

Climbing a Hill

Hiking is like a roller coaster.
It's not just one long climb
and then the ride is over.

The dizzying drop after that first
climb sets in motion a wild journey—
bends, curves, smaller hills
that take me by surprise.

I don't want the ride—the climb—
to ever end. All too soon, the coaster
car glides to a stop, like loping down
that last stretch of steep hill.

A sense of accomplishment
dares me to climb again.

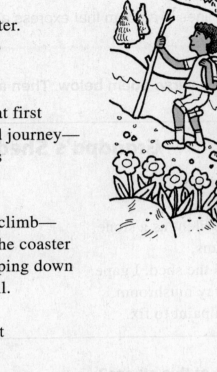

Answer the questions about the text.

1. How do you know this is free verse poetry?

_____

2. How is the text arranged on the page?

_____

_____

3. What other literary elements are used in the text?

_____

_____

_____

4. What feelings does the speaker express?

_____

_____

_____

Name _____

> **Meter,** or **rhythm,** is a repeating pattern of stressed and unstressed syllables.
>
> **Stanzas** are groups of lines in a poem that express a key idea.

Read the lines of the free verse poem below. Then answer the questions.

Grandpa's Shed

My grandpa is a mountain,
    Brooding, looming, tall.
I stand in his shadow, silent as a stone.
Rattling rusty paint cans,
    He gestures toward the shed. I gape.
That shed's a squat gray mushroom,
    Needing more than paint to fix.

1. **What is the key idea of this stanza?**

   _____

2. **What syllables are stressed in the first three lines of this stanza?**

   _____

3. **Write another stanza for this poem that uses irregular meter.**

   _____

   _____

   _____

   _____

Name _____

Read each passage. Underline the similes and metaphors. Then explain the author's meaning in your own words.

1. My grandpa is a mountain, / Brooding, looming, tall.

   _____

2. I stand in his shadow, silent as a stone.

   _____

3. That shed's a squat gray mushroom,

   _____

4. The old man's hands are vises, / Prying open paint cans lightning fast.

   _____

5. My words explode like fireworks.

   _____

6. Anticipating anger, my mouth shuts like a trap.

   _____

7. We share the shed like one vast canvas

   _____

Name _____

The suffixes *-ance* **and** *-ence* **can mean "an action or act" or "the state of."**
Read each sentence and write the word that has the suffix *-ance* **or** *-ence*.
Use what you know about the meaning of the suffix to write the meaning of
the word.

1. The people in attendance cheered when their team scored the winning goal.

   _____

2. My brother and sister enjoyed the choir performance last weekend.

   _____

3. Our dependence on electricity is fueling a search for new types of energy.

   _____

4. The barking dogs created quite a disturbance in the neighborhood.

   _____

5. The sudden appearance of the fox startled us.

   _____

6. A good leader should have the ability to inspire confidence and trust.

   _____

7. Their idea to create a new park on the empty lot was met with great resistance.

   _____

8. It will take persistence to achieve your physical fitness goals.

   _____

Name _____

Evidence is details and examples from a text that support a writer's ideas. The student who wrote the paragraph below cited evidence to show how the poet used sensory language to convey an experience.

Topic sentence ⟶ In "Grandpa's Shed," the poet used sensory language to show what the speaker experienced when painting the shed with Grandpa. Grandpa is "brooding, looming, tall." I can

Evidence ⟶ clearly picture a tall and grumpy grandpa. "Rattling" helps me imagine the sound of Grandpa carrying paint cans. The words "vises, prying" help me imagine how strong Grandpa's

Concluding statement ⟶ hands must be. All of these words help me understand what the speaker experienced when painting with Grandpa.

Write a paragraph about a poem. Show how the poet used sensory language to convey an experience. Cite words and phrases from the poem that helped you imagine the look, smell, taste, feel, or sound of something.

Write a topic sentence: _____

_____

Cite evidence from the text: _____

_____

_____

_____

End with a concluding statement: _____

_____

Name _____

A. Read the draft model. Use the questions that follow the draft to help you think about how you can add sensory language to make the writing more interesting.

Draft Model

The word *imagine* is the best.
I like the way it looks.
It sounds nicer than the rest.

---

1. Which words could you use to create a clearer image of the word *imagine*?

2. Which words can you add to explain why the sound of the word is pleasing?

3. What other sensory details would help readers share the writer's experience?

B. Now revise the draft by rewriting sentences to include sensory details and to describe an experience or subject for the reader.

_____

_____

_____

_____

_____

_____

_____

_____

_____

_____

Name _____

| disdain | prospect | focused | superb |
| genius | stunned | perspective | transition |

Finish each sentence using the vocabulary word provided.

1. (perspective) We looked at the problem from _____

_____

2. (disdain) When he said he didn't like any of my favorite things, _____

_____

3. (superb) She liked all the food, but _____

_____

4. (transition) My little sister will soon _____

_____

5. (genius) We each have our own talents, but _____

_____

6. (stunned) When the best runner slipped on the track, _____

_____

7. (prospect) After working hard all year, _____

_____

8. (focused) The dog was sitting at the window _____

_____

Name _____

Read the selection. Complete the compare and contrast graphic organizer.

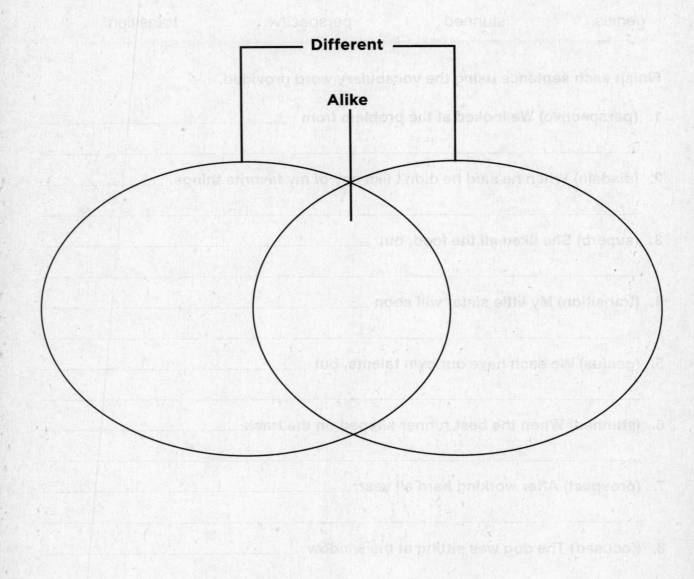

Different

Alike

Name _____

Read the passage. Use the make predictions strategy to help you understand what you are reading.

Bringing Home Laddie

12	"Papa, let's go!" Sofia was dressed and waiting on the shabby wooden
	porch. Her father couldn't hear her. He was in the neighbor's garden,
24	digging up an ancient tree stump. Sofia shifted her feet and picked at the
38	peeling paint on the railing. The sun hammered down on the porch, so
51	that it was not merely hot, but sweltering. It would serve Papa right if she
66	melted away like the Wicked Witch of the West. Why should Sofia have to
80	wait? Why couldn't their neighbor, Mrs. Stone, wait instead? Then Papa
91	could drive Sofia to the animal shelter now to adopt her new dog.
104	Sofia peered into the shadows of the house. "Mom," she yelled, "Papa
116	promised we could go early. Do I have to walk?" She could imagine how
130	unhappy she'd look—just another stray dog trudging dejectedly down
140	the road.
142	Her mother came to the door, a damp dish towel in her hand. "Sofia,
156	come help me." Sofia stayed where she was, as rooted as the neighbor's
169	tree stump. "Standing here won't make your father finish any sooner. If
181	you help me, he'll be here before you know it."
191	Sofia gave a sigh of profound suffering and followed her mother
202	through the cool house into the spotless, lemony kitchen. She leaned
213	against the counter and dried the dishes her mother handed her—along
225	with a reminder of the promise she'd made to take care of the dog herself.
240	"I know, Mom, I know," Sofia whined. To her surprise, by the time the
254	dishes were dry, Papa was back. The time really had passed quickly, just as
268	Mom had said it would.
273	When Sofia and her parents arrived at the shelter, an attendant escorted
285	them to the dogs' quarters, a glaring concrete courtyard lined with tiny
297	cages on all four sides. Its smell was revolting—a mixture of mouthwash
310	and Papa's old fishing bucket.

Name _____

"Go look at them, Sweetie," said her father with a smile. Sofia was already heading toward one of the cages. As she neared it, the gaunt gray dog inside bared its teeth, backing away and growling. Sofia stared at it blankly. Didn't the dog like her? Maybe none of them would! Tears crowded her eyes, making them ache.

The attendant, who had followed Sofia, offered an explanation, "That poor thing's just skin and bones, and she's terrified of people. I think she's been mistreated. Let's go meet Laddie." Sofia looked back at the forlorn little dog, and she could see now how sad it looked.

Laddie was larger than the first dog, and his black and white fur was shaggier. When he saw Sofia, he rushed to the front of his cage, lifted his front legs, and scrabbled at the wire with his forepaws. One of his eyes was sky blue, and the other was chocolate brown. "You can pet him," the woman said to Sofia. "He won't bite." Sofia reached toward Laddie's smiling muzzle. The little sheepdog whined and gently licked her fingers. Sofia felt a tug at her heart and realized that Laddie had just slipped a leash over it.

The attendant took Laddie from his cage. He rolled onto his back, wagging his tail and gazing devotedly at Sofia. She rubbed his belly. The attendant showed how to hold his leash in two hands when she walked Laddie and reminded her to clean up after him. "Never leave his mess on other people's lawns," the attendant instructed. Sofia nodded, smiling.

As soon as they arrived home, Sofia got bowls of water and food for Laddie. She set them on a rubber mat on the kitchen floor and watched while Laddie ate. When he was done, she washed his food bowl and put it back on the shelf. "Well," said her mother with a proud smile, "it seems like you'll be looking after someone else for a change." Sofia grinned, petting the head of her contented dog.

Stuffing some plastic bags into her pocket, she picked up Laddie's leash. "Want to go meet Mrs. Stone?" As Laddie bounded beside her, his tail waved hello to all his new neighbors.

Name _____

A. Reread the passage and answer the questions.

1. Contrast the first dog and Laddie. How are they different?

_____

_____

2. How does Sofia change from the beginning of the story to the end?

_____

_____

3. What causes the change in Sofia?

_____

_____

4. How are the settings of the animal shelter and Sofia's kitchen different?

_____

_____

B. Work with a partner. Read the passage aloud. Pay attention to expression. Stop after one minute. Fill out the chart.

	Words Read	–	Number of Errors	=	Words Correct Score
First Read		–		=	
Second Read		–		=	

Name _____

The Spelling Bee

Gabe stood in the wings of the high school auditorium. The stage was huge, with chairs for 45 students. There were 3,000 people in the audience. "This is very different from our school's auditorium," he thought. "Ours holds only 300 people, and our stage isn't big enough to hold a fly." Gabe had won his school's spelling bee, but he doubted he would do well here. "I'll do the best I can," Gabe said to himself as he stepped onto the stage and focused on the spelling bee. By the end of the day, Gabe had made it to the state finals, and he felt a lot better about himself.

Answer the questions about the text.

1. **How do you know this text is realistic fiction? What makes the characters, events, and dialogue realistic?**

   _____

   _____

2. **Write an example of figurative language found in the text. Explain why it is figurative language.**

   _____

   _____

   _____

3. **Who is the narrator of the story? Explain how you know.**

   _____

   _____

4. **Write a descriptive detail from the text that tells how Gabe felt after the spelling bee. How does this detail help you experience the text as realistic?**

   _____

   _____

Name _____

Read each sentence. Underline the context clues in the sentence that help you define each word in bold. Then, in your own words, write the definition of the word in bold.

1. The sun hammered down on the porch, so that it was not merely hot, but **sweltering**.

_____

2. Its smell was **revolting**—a mixture of mouthwash and Papa's old fishing bucket.

_____

3. As she neared it, the **gaunt** gray dog inside bared its teeth, backing away and growling. . . . The attendant, who had followed Sofia, offered an explanation. "That poor thing's just skin and bones, and she's terrified of people."

_____

4. Sofia looked back at the **forlorn** little dog, and she could see now how sad it looked.

_____

5. As soon as he saw Sofia, he rushed to the front of his cage, lifted his front legs, and scrabbled at the wire with his **forepaws**.

_____

Name _____

A. Add the suffix in parentheses to the word in bold.

New Word

1. (less) **weight** _____

2. (ist) **violin** _____

3. (ion) **express** _____

4. (ist) **art** _____

5. (ful) **forget** _____

B. Circle the suffix in each word. Then write a definition of the word based on the suffix.

6. narration _____

7. thoughtful _____

8. biologist _____

9. eruption _____

10. limitless _____

Name _____

Evidence is details and examples from a text that support a writer's opinion. The student who wrote the paragraph below cited evidence to show how well the author used details to show setting.

Topic sentence → I think the author of "Bringing Home Laddie" did a good job of using details to show different settings. At the beginning, Sofia waits on a wooden porch at home. It is sweltering. Then Sofia goes inside to help her mother in the kitchen. It is cool, spotless, and lemony. Finally, Sofia goes to the shelter to get a dog. The shelter has a concrete courtyard lined with cages on all sides. It smells like mouthwash and a fishing bucket. I can clearly imagine each place. I think the author did a good job of using details to show setting.

Evidence →

Concluding statement →

Write a paragraph about a realistic fiction story. Cite evidence from the text to support your opinion as to how well the author used details to show different settings.

Write a topic sentence: _____

_____

Cite evidence from the text: _____

_____

_____

_____

_____

End with a concluding statement: _____

_____

Name _____

A. Read the draft model. Use the questions that follow the draft to help you think about how you can change the opening to get the reader's attention.

Draft Model

I had waited a long time for a trip to the water park. The biggest slide was really high, but it was supposed to be fun.

1. What descriptive words could you add to the first sentence to make the reader want to know more about the writer's trip?

2. What details could you add to tell how the writer felt about going on this trip?

3. What details could you add to describe what the slide is like?

4. What details could you add to make the ride on the slide seem interesting?

B. Now revise the draft by adding details to create a strong opening.

_____

_____

_____

_____

_____

_____

_____

_____

Name _____

| assume | guarantee | nominate | obviously |
| sympathy | weakling | rely | supportive |

Write a complete sentence to answer each question below. In your answer, use the vocabulary word in bold.

1. Why is being **supportive** a good quality in a friend? _____

   _____

2. What might make you **nominate** someone for class president? _____

   _____

3. What do you **assume** when an expert speaks about his or her work? _____

   _____

4. What is true about a person who is **obviously** rushing somewhere? _____

   _____

5. What kind of person has **sympathy** for other people's problems? _____

   _____

6. What is something that can help **guarantee** that you will get good grades? _____

   _____

7. Why wouldn't a **weakling** make a very good weightlifter? _____

   _____

8. What is a way that you can **rely** upon a good umbrella? _____

   _____

Name _____

Read the selection. Complete the compare and contrast graphic organizer.

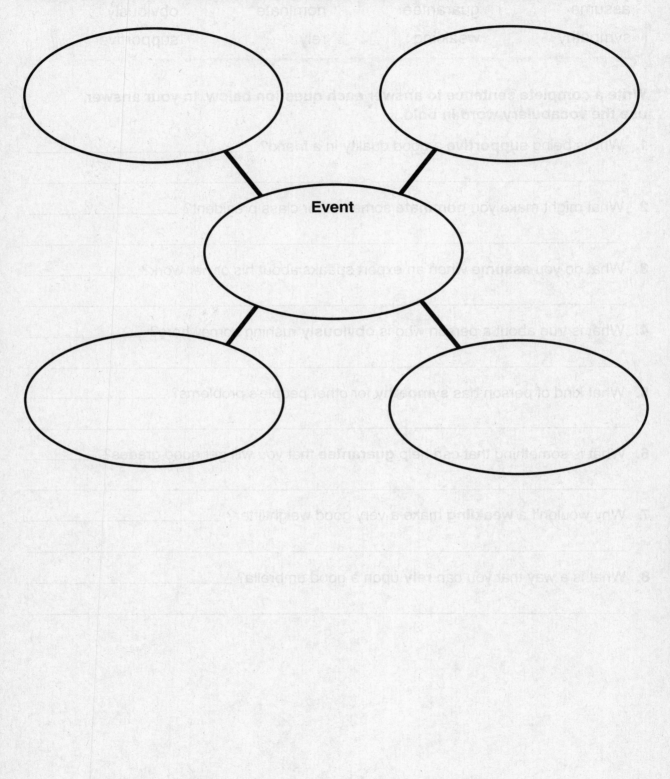

Event

Name _____

Read the passage. Use the make predictions strategy to check your understanding.

Nancy's First Interview

	Nancy poured herself a bowl of cornflakes as her father finished a
12	telephone call. "You're really putting me on the spot," he said to the
25	person at the other end of the line. "I already have a commitment today,
39	Jim." After a few moments, Mr. Jenson sighed and hung up the telephone.
52	Nancy looked up from her breakfast, preparing for bad news.
62	Her father gave her a sad smile. "I'm really sorry, Nance, but I have
76	to work today. We'll have to reschedule our fishing trip." Mr. Jenson was
89	a reporter for the city newspaper. After the stock market crash of 1929,
102	his newspaper had laid off most of the reporters. Four years later, they
115	still had only a skeleton crew. He was glad to have a job, but he was
131	overworked and underpaid.
134	Nancy shrugged, trying not to look too upset. She wished she could do
147	something to comfort her dad. The last thing she wanted was to make him
161	feel guilty. "It's okay, Dad," she said, forcing a cheerful smile.
172	"The worst part is that our photographers are on other assignments,"
183	he grumbled, shaking his head. He paused for a moment, lost in thought.
196	"Nancy," he said, "do you remember when I showed you how to use
209	my camera?" She nodded. "Do you think you could help me today? I
222	can't carry all of the equipment by myself, and we'd get to spend some
236	time together."
238	Nancy jumped up from her chair and ran to her bedroom to change out
252	of her fishing clothes. "Make tracks," her dad called down the hallway.
264	"We're in a hurry!"

Name _____

As Mr. Jenson navigated their car out of town, he told Nancy about the assignment. They were going to interview the Carter family, migrant workers who had moved from Oklahoma to California in search of work. Also known as "Okies," these families were escaping a life of drought and poverty.

During the Great Depression of the 1930s, migrant workers packed their few belongings and headed for California.

Mr. Jenson pulled up to a crooked shanty on the edge of a farm. A lanky man and a rotund woman greeted them.

Nancy and her father followed the Carters into the shabby house. All of their belongings were in one room: two dingy mattresses, a wobbly kitchen table with four mismatched chairs, and a small camping stove.

The adults sat around the table and Nancy hovered nervously near her father. She felt self-conscious; her family's small house seemed like a mansion compared to this place.

Mr. Jenson started the interview. "What brought you folks to California?" he asked, opening his notebook.

"Work," Mr. Carter said. He explained that they had owned a farm in Oklahoma, but lost it when costs rose. "Upkeep cost an arm and a leg, and the drought killed our chances of a good crop."

"Do you miss home?" Nancy blurted. She looked down, embarrassed. She knew better than to interrupt, but her father gave her an encouraging smile.

"There's nothing to miss," Mrs. Carter said, shrugging. "The only thing we have left in this world is each other."

Nancy was bursting with questions, and the Carters answered them all. She realized that her family wasn't that much different from the Carters. When times were tough, families had to support one another.

After the interview, Nancy's father helped her set up the camera so she could take a few photos. Mr. Carter nodded at her and said, "You've got a good little reporter there."

Mr. Jenson grinned and ruffled Nancy's hair. "I taught her everything she knows," he said. "She's a chip off the old block."

Name _____

A. Reread the passage and answer the questions.

1. Why does Nancy go with Mr. Jenson on his newspaper assignment?

_____

_____

2. How does the Carters' home contrast with the Jensons' house?

_____

_____

3. What similarities does Nancy see when she compares her own family with the Carters?

_____

_____

4. When Mr. Jenson says that Nancy is a "chip off the old block," is he comparing or contrasting the two of them? Explain.

_____

_____

B. Work with a partner. Read the passage aloud. Pay attention to expression and phrasing. Stop after one minute. Fill out the chart.

	Words Read	–	Number of Errors	=	Words Correct Score
First Read		–		=	
Second Read		–		=	

Name _____

Afternoons Alone

Rusty moped around the empty house. Grandpa had been helping to build tanks at the factory since America declared war against Japan. Without him, there was nobody to fish with. There was no one to talk with in the afternoon.

Yesterday, his friend Corey had told Rusty, "Every day, after school, I clean house and do chores. Then, when Mom returns home from the tank factory, we can have some fun time together."

"How keen it will be when the war ends!" exclaimed Rusty.

"We'll have lots of family time then," Corey said excitedly.

Rusty eyed the dirty windows in his house and said to himself, "Maybe I can help with some chores, too."

Answer the questions about the text.

1. **How do you know that this text is historical fiction?**

   _____

   _____

2. **What events in the text are typical of the time period in which the text is set?**

   _____

   _____

3. **Write an example of dialect in the text and tell what it means.**

   _____

   _____

Name _____

Read each passage. Underline the idiom in each one. Then, on the lines below the passage, restate the idiom in your own words.

1. "You're really putting me on the spot," he said to the person at the other end of the line. "I already have a commitment today, Jim."

   _____

   _____

2. After the stock market crash of 1929, his newspaper had laid off most of the reporters. Four years later, they still had only a skeleton crew. He was glad to have a job, but he was overworked and underpaid.

   _____

   _____

3. Nancy jumped up from her chair and ran to her bedroom to change out of her fishing clothes. "Make tracks," her dad called down the hallway. "We're in a hurry!"

   _____

   _____

4. He explained that they had owned a farm in Oklahoma, but lost it when costs rose. "Upkeep cost an arm and a leg, and the drought killed our chances of a good crop."

   _____

   _____

5. Mr. Jenson grinned and ruffled Nancy's hair. "I taught her everything she knows," he said. "She's a chip off the old block."

   _____

   _____

Name _____

stationery	presents	pray	colonel	manner
pier	council	presence	waist	suite

A. Read each pair of words below. Circle the word that is a homophone of a word from the box above. Then write a word from the box to form a homophone pair.

1. sweet, sweat _____

2. stationing, stationary _____

3. count, counsel _____

4. manor, mansion _____

5. kernel, color _____

B. Choose three homophone pairs from above. Write a sentence using each pair of words.

6. _____

_____

7. _____

_____

8. _____

_____

Name _____

Evidence is details and examples from a text that support a writer's ideas. The student who wrote the paragraph below cited evidence to explain how the author developed the setting of a historical fiction story.

Topic sentence →   In "Nancy's First Interview," the author uses details to show that the story takes place in America during the 1930s. The author includes the detail that the newspaper

Evidence → laid off people after the stock market crash in 1929. I know that this was a real event. Mr. Jenson and Nancy are going to interview a family that had moved from Oklahoma to California in search of work. I know that during the 1930s many families moved to California to find work. These

Concluding statement → details show that the story takes place in America during the 1930s.

Write a paragraph about a historical fiction story. Cite evidence from the text to show how the author used details to develop the setting.

Write a topic sentence: _____

_____

Cite evidence from the text: _____

_____

_____

_____

_____

End with a concluding statement: _____

_____

Name _____

A. Read the draft model. Use the questions that follow the draft to help you think about adding transitions to help connect ideas.

Draft Model

We help clean up the local park. I pick up trash. My mom gathers items for recycling. We take everything to the waste collection site. We head home.

---

1. How are the ideas in the second and third sentences of the paragraph related?

2. What transition words could you add to the third sentence to link it to the second sentence?

3. What transition could you place at the beginning of the last sentence to show when it happens?

B. Now revise the draft by adding transitions to help connect ideas and to help readers follow what happens at the park.

Name _____

| atmosphere | variations | receding | noticeably |
| stability | decays | gradual | impact |

Finish each sentence using the vocabulary word provided.

1. **(atmosphere) The weather balloon they launched** _____

_____

2. **(decays) When food sits out for too long,** _____

_____

3. **(gradual) The airplane began** _____

_____

4. **(impact) People can have** _____

_____

5. **(noticeably) The house was** _____

_____

6. **(receding) I noticed** _____

_____

7. **(stability) Three wheels give a tricycle** _____

_____

8. **(variations) We were amazed to see** _____

_____

Name _____

Read the selection. Complete the compare and contrast graphic organizer.

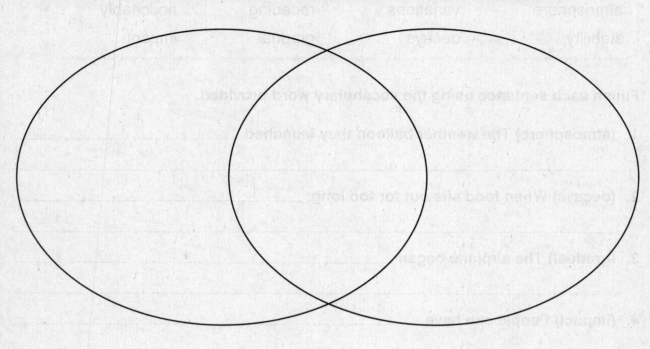

Name _____

Read the passage. Use the ask and answer questions strategy to help you understand what you read.

Of Floods and Fish

	The Mississippi River flows more than two thousand miles from
10	Minnesota to the Gulf of Mexico. Every few years, it floods. In April and
24	May, 2011, a combination of melting snow and falling rain along the upper
37	part of the river caused the lower part of the river to overrun its banks.
52	Floods cause widespread destruction. Floodwaters damage and
59	sometimes knock down buildings. They destroy farmland and animal
68	habitats. With nowhere to live, the animals often move into populated
79	areas. What about the fish? Because they live in water, shouldn't a flood
92	be good for them? As it turns out, floods can hurt fish populations just as
107	they harm many animals that live on the land.
116	**The Dead Zone**
119	The Mississippi floodwaters proved most detrimental to the fish and
129	other ocean life in the Gulf of Mexico. The Mississippi River is made
142	of fresh water. The Gulf is made of salt water. The extra river water
156	that flowed into the Gulf endangered the native saltwater fish. More
167	harmful, though, were the pollutants the river water carried with it. As the
180	swollen Mississippi washed over farmland, it picked up the fertilizer and
191	pesticides that farmers had used on the land and crops. These chemicals
203	are poisonous to ocean life. The river then dumped these poisons into
215	the Gulf. The extra river water and the farm runoff created a dead zone
229	along the coast. A dead zone is an area of water that does not have enough
245	oxygen to support life.

Name _____

Threat of Invasion

The flooding of the Mississippi River posed a different threat to the fish that lived in it: the spread of an invasive species called Asian carp. Asian carp were brought to fish farms in the United States in the 1970s. A flood washed some of them from the farms into parts of the Mississippi River. In these places, the carp took over, threatening the native fish. When the Mississippi flooded again in 2011, scientists feared that the Asian carp would spread even farther.

Aaron Roeth Photography

Supporting Life

Despite these problems, though, the freshwater fish that lived in the Mississippi River fared much better than those in the Gulf. For these Mississippi River fish, the extra river water provided advantages that helped them breed and survive.

As the river grew, so did the available habitat for the river's fish. River fish usually stay along the edges of a river, where the water is slower and shallower. The underwater plants and overhanging branches in these areas provide protection and food. When the Mississippi flooded, it increased the amount of shallow water on the river's edges. This gave the fish more water to swim in and more places to hide from predators. The spreading water also introduced more food. These factors improved the fish's chances of survival.

The expanded habitat provided more benefits than extra hiding places and food sources. It also created more areas for fish to spawn. The newly flooded areas allowed fish to lay eggs safely, away from predators and other dangers. This, in turn, meant more new fish hatched successfully.

If the flooding of the Mississippi teaches any lesson, it is that changes in the environment can affect living things in surprising ways. Despite its harmful effects, some animals benefitted from the change.

Name _____

A. Reread the passage and answer the questions.

1. What comparison does the phrase *just as* indicate in the second paragraph?

   _____

   _____

2. In what way are the main ideas of the sections called "The Dead Zone" and "Threat of Invasion" alike?

   _____

   _____

   _____

3. Are the ideas in the section "Supporting Life" similar to or different from the ideas in the previous two sections? Explain.

   _____

   _____

   _____

B. Work with a partner. Read the passage aloud. Pay attention to rate. Stop after one minute. Fill out the chart.

	Words Read	–	Number of Errors	=	Words Correct Score
First Read		–		=	
Second Read		–		=	

Name _____

Moths and Changes in Weather

Scientists study moths to see how quickly they can adapt to climate change. Some moths adapt better than others. Some species of moths need cool weather and move north when the weather gets warmer. Moths already living in cool areas may not be able to find a cooler place to go. Warm weather affects the food caterpillars eat. Some caterpillars adapt to climate change and food supplies by hatching earlier or later than usual. It is hard to predict how climate change will affect moths over time.

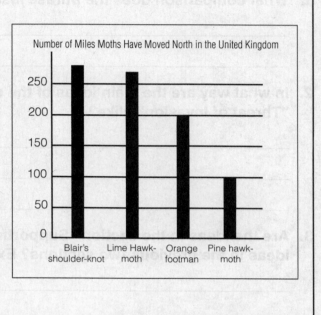

Answer the questions about the text.

1. How do you know this is expository text?

   _____

   _____

2. Is the heading a strong heading for the text? Why or why not?

   _____

   _____

3. What text feature does this text include?

   _____

4. What do you learn from the text feature and its title?

   _____

   _____

Name _____

Read each passage. Underline the context clues that help you figure out the meaning of each word in bold. Then write the word's meaning on the line.

1. Every few years, it floods. In April and May, 2011, a combination of melting snow and falling rain along the upper part of the river caused the lower part of the river to **overrun** its banks.

    _____

2. Floods cause widespread destruction. Floodwaters damage and sometimes knock down buildings. They destroy farmland and animal **habitats**. With nowhere to live, the animals often move into populated areas.

    _____

3. The Mississippi floodwaters proved most **detrimental** to the fish and other ocean life in the Gulf of Mexico. The Mississippi River is made of fresh water. The Gulf is made of salt water. The extra river water that flowed into the Gulf endangered the native saltwater fish. More harmful, though, were the pollutants the river water carried with it.

    _____

4. As the swollen Mississippi washed over farmland, it picked up the fertilizer and **pesticides** that farmers had used on the land and crops. These chemicals are poisonous to ocean life.

    _____

5. The flooding of the Mississippi River posed a different threat to the fish that lived in it: the spread of an **invasive** species called Asian carp. Asian carp were brought to fish farms in the United States in the 1970s. A flood washed some of the carp from the farms into parts of the Mississippi River. In these places, the carp took over, threatening the native fish.

    _____

6. The expanded habitat provided more benefits than extra hiding places and food sources. It also created more areas for fish to **spawn**. The newly flooded areas allowed the fish to lay their eggs safely, away from predators and other dangers.

    _____

Name _____

> *dis-* means "not," "absence of," or "opposite of"
>
> *in-* means "not" or "opposite of"
>
> *mis-* means "wrong" or "not"
>
> *pre-* means "before"

Add a prefix from the box to complete the word in each sentence below. Use context clues to help you decide which prefix to use.

1. She will _____ wash the fabric to make sure it will not shrink.

2. Please remember to _____ connect from the Internet before you turn off the computer.

3. Their visitors will stay for an _____ definite amount of time.

4. He felt some _____ comfort when he hurt his leg.

5. If you do not speak clearly, they will _____ understand your directions.

6. She has little money, so she hopes to find an _____ expensive gift.

7. The teacher will _____ view the video before showing it to the class.

8. A friendship can be harmed if there is _____ trust between two people.

9. Always _____ heat the oven before you bake bread.

10. I _____ approve of the way they are behaving.

Name _____

Evidence is details and examples from a text that support a writer's ideas. The student who wrote the paragraph below cited evidence to show how the author compared and contrasted information to explain the topic.

Topic sentence →   In "Of Floods and Fish," the author compares the effects of a Mississippi River flood to show that flooding can be harmful and helpful. After a river floods, chemicals from

Evidence → farmlands can be carried down the river into the Gulf. This can harm fish that live there. The author compares this to what happens to fish in the Mississippi River. The flood creates a bigger habitat. This helps fish survive. By

Concluding statement → comparing and contrasting these effects, the author shows that flooding can be helpful and harmful to fish.

Write a paragraph about the text you chose. Cite text evidence to analyze how the author compared and contrasted information to explain a topic.

Write a topic sentence: _____

_____

Cite evidence from the text: _____

_____

_____

_____

_____

End with a concluding statement: _____

_____

Name _____

A. Read the draft model. Use the questions that follow the draft to help you think about how you can add details to support the topic.

Draft Model

Our region is experiencing a drought. It hasn't rained in a long time. Things aren't growing. Everything is brown.

---

1. What kinds of details can you add to develop the topic?

2. What facts or concrete details could be added to explain the first sentence?

3. What other details would show how the landscape looks?

B. Now revise the draft by adding details to support the topic and develop ideas about the drought.

_____

_____

_____

_____

_____

_____

_____

_____

Name _____

> approximately   astronomical   calculation   criteria
>
> diameter   evaluate   orbit   spheres

Use each pair of vocabulary words in a single sentence.

1. spheres, diameter

_____

_____

2. evaluate, criteria

_____

_____

3. astronomical, orbit

_____

_____

4. calculation, approximately

_____

_____

Name _____

Read the selection. Complete the cause and effect graphic organizer.

Cause	→	Effect
	→	
	→	
	→	
	→	

Name _____

Read the passage. Use the ask and answer questions strategy to check your understanding as you read.

Is There Life Out There?

11	"Is there life out there?" is a question scientists who study astrobiology are trying to answer. They look for life in space. In recent
24	years, they have turned their attention to Europa, one of Jupiter's four
36	largest moons.
38	Europa is a little smaller than Earth's moon and is covered by a sheet of
53	ice. Its surface is too cold and exposed to too much radiation for anything
67	to live there. Scientists want to know what lies beneath the ice, for that is
82	where any life on Europa would most likely be.
91	**The Necessities of Life**
95	For years, scientists believed all life on Earth depended on energy
106	from the sun. During a process called photosynthesis, plants use energy
117	from sunlight to make food and to release oxygen into the atmosphere.
129	Aerobic creatures rely on that oxygen to breathe. In addition to providing
141	the fuel for photosynthesis, sunlight also provides the necessary
150	warmth for life to survive. Scientists believed life could not survive in
162	extreme temperatures.
164	Scientists also believed that all food chains led back to photosynthesis
175	and the food produced by plants. Recent discoveries, however, have
185	changed the way scientists think about life. They have discovered tube-
196	shaped, worm-like creatures and other animals living around hydrothermal
204	vents on the ocean floor. These newfound creatures do not rely on the sun
218	or plants for food and energy.

Name _____

The animals living around hydrothermal vents eat a form of bacteria that live on or below the ocean floor. The bacteria get energy during a process called chemosynthesis. Hydrothermal vents spit warm water filled with chemicals from inside the earth. The bacteria use these chemicals the way plants on the surface use sunlight: as a source of food and energy.

New Possibilities

The discovery of chemosynthetic life changed the way astrobiologists think about life in space. No longer do they have to look only for planets with sunlight and oxygen. Based on Earth's example, planets with oceans and hydrothermal vents might also support life. Based on these discoveries, Europa began to seem like a place where life might exist.

Europa has an oxygen-rich atmosphere, but the oxygen is not produced by photosynthesis. Europa is too far from the sun and too cold to support photosynthetic life. Its surface temperature is usually more than 200 degrees below zero Fahrenheit.

Europa does have oceans. In fact, Europa appears to have more oceans than Earth does. The ice on this moon's surface covers what appears to be moving liquid water. Do these oceans contain hydrothermal vents? Scientists do not yet know. If they do, the oceans of Europa might support chemosynthetic life. Only a space mission to Europa would tell for certain.

Until then, scientists are studying the closest possible environment they can find on Earth: Lake Vostok in Antarctica. Like Europa's oceans, Lake Vostok exists miles beneath a frozen surface. It does not receive direct sunlight, either. Therefore, like Europa, the lake cannot support photosynthetic life. If scientists find life in the lake, it would support the idea that there might also be life on Europa.

Name _____

A. Reread the passage and answer the questions.

1. What details from the first two paragraphs help explain why astrobiologists are interested in Europa, one of Jupiter's moons?

   _____

   _____

2. What discovery on Earth caused scientists to become more interested in Europa?

   _____

   _____

   _____

3. What is the scientists' main reason for studying Lake Vostok in Antarctica? What effect might their research have?

   _____

   _____

   _____

   _____

B. Work with a partner. Read the passage aloud. Pay attention to accuracy. Stop after one minute. Fill out the chart.

	Words Read	–	Number of Errors	=	Words Correct Score
First Read		–		=	
Second Read		–		=	

Name _____

Seeing the Light

In 1803, Thomas Young made a discovery about light. He found that when light from two sources overlapped, it made a pattern of bright light and darkness. He thought light acted like a wave: the bright areas were created when two light waves matched up; the dark areas were created when two light waves did not match. His theory led to future discoveries about light.

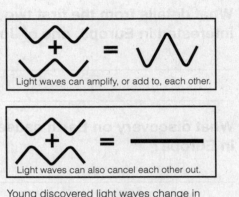

Light waves can amplify, or add to, each other.

Light waves can also cancel each other out.

Young discovered light waves change in brightness when they overlap.

Answer the questions about the text.

1. **What genre of text is this? How do you know?**

   _____

   _____

2. **What text features does this text include?**

   _____

   _____

3. **How does the title relate to the main idea?**

   _____

   _____

4. **How does the graphic text feature help you better understand the text?**

   _____

   _____

Name _____

aero = air	*chemo* = chemical	*sphaira* = globe, ball
atmos = vapor, steam	*hydro* = water	*syntithenai* = making or putting together
astro = star	*logy* = the study of	*therme* = heat
bio = life	*photo* = light	

Read each passage below. For each word in bold, write the Greek root or roots from the box above. Use the Greek roots and context clues to write the word's meaning.

1. "Is there life out there?" is a question scientists who study **astrobiology** are trying to answer. They look for life in space.

   Greek root(s): _____

   Meaning: _____

2. During a process called **photosynthesis**, plants use energy from sunlight to make food.

   Greek root(s): _____

   Meaning: _____

3. Plants make food and release oxygen into the **atmosphere**.

   Greek root(s): _____

   Meaning: _____

4. **Aerobic** creatures rely on that oxygen to breathe.

   Greek root(s): _____

   Meaning: _____

5. The animals living around **hydrothermal** vents eat a form of bacteria that live on or below the ocean floor.

   Greek root(s): _____

   Meaning: _____

Name _____

A. Read each sentence. Write the word with the suffix *-less* or *-ness* on the line. Then circle the suffix.

1. The owls went hunting under the cover of darkness. _____

2. The fearless police officers raced to the rescue. _____

3. "I will not tolerate this foolishness," our teacher said. _____

4. Were you filled with sadness when your team lost the game? _____

5. The photographer captured the fullness of the moon. _____

6. The situation seemed hopeless, but we kept trying. _____

B. Add the suffix *-less* or *-ness* to the word in parentheses. Write the new sentence on the line.

7. Our boat drifted for hours on the (motion) sea.

   _____

8. Did you see the (fierce) in the tiger's eyes?

   _____

9. The spider looked (harm), but I decided not to touch it.

   _____

10. My parents and I have a (fond) for picnics in the woods.

    _____

Name _____

Evidence is details and examples from a text that support a writer's ideas. The student who wrote the paragraph below cited evidence that explains how an author clearly shows a cause-and-effect relationship between an event and ideas.

Topic sentence $\longrightarrow$ In "Is There Life Out There?" the author clearly shows the cause-and-effect relationship between a discovery and new ideas about life on planets. The author describes the

Evidence $\longrightarrow$ discovery of animals that can live around hydrothermal vents in the ocean. This caused scientists to change the way they think about how life gets energy on Earth. The discovery also made scientists think that other planets with hydrothermal vents might also support life. The author

Concluding statement $\longrightarrow$ clearly shows the cause-and-effect relationship between a discovery and new ideas about life on planets.

Write a paragraph about the text you have chosen. Tell how the author clearly shows cause-and-effect relationships between events and ideas. Cite evidence from the text.

Write a topic sentence: _____

_____

Cite evidence from the text: _____

_____

_____

_____

_____

End with a concluding statement: _____

_____

Name _____

A. Read the draft model. Use the questions that follow the draft to help you think about how to add related ideas and delete unrelated ideas to create a stronger paragraph.

Draft Model

The best way to learn about space is with a telescope. You can see what the surface of Earth's moon looks like. The moon is not a planet.

---

1. What is the main topic of this paragraph?

2. How might you describe a telescope? For example, are there different types?

3. What can you learn from studying the surface of the moon?

4. What idea in the paragraph is unrelated to the rest of the paragraph?

B. Now revise the draft by adding related ideas and deleting unrelated ideas to make a strong paragraph.

Name _____

| agricultural | declined | disorder | identify |
| probable | thrive | unexpected | widespread |

Finish each sentence using the vocabulary word provided.

1. **(identify)** He learned how _____
   _____ .

2. **(unexpected)** The outcome of the game _____
   _____ .

3. **(declined)** The population of the city _____
   _____ .

4. **(thrive)** The plants in the shade _____
   _____ .

5. **(disorder)** Our neighbor's dog has _____
   _____ .

6. **(agricultural)** Our country's ability to grow large amounts of food _____
   _____ .

7. **(widespread)** Lack of rainfall for several months _____
   _____ .

8. **(probable)** Scientists say _____
   _____ .

Name _____

Read the selection. Complete the author's point of view graphic organizer.

Details	Author's Point of View

Name _____

Read the two passages. Use the ask and answer questions strategy to
check your understanding as you read.

WHAT IS THE FUTURE OF THE RAIN FORESTS?

Rain Forests Support People

4	*People must make economic use of the rain forests.*
13	The removal of rain forest trees has some negative consequences, but it
25	is necessary for the survival of people and national economies. Therefore,
36	it is not practical or desirable to try to stop the cutting of all rain forest
52	trees. A better plan is to make economic use of rain forests.
64	Farming in the Rain Forests
69	In most cases, when part of a rain forest is cut down, subsistence
82	agriculture takes its place. Subsistence agriculture is farming or ranching
92	that produces only enough for a family to meet its everyday needs. The
105	families need these farms or ranches in order to survive.
115	Commercial Use of Rain Forests
120	Commercial activities also play a role in the use of rain forest land.
133	Lumber from rain forest trees is used to make furniture, flooring, and
145	paper. Many countries buy beef that comes from cattle ranches on former
157	rain forest land. Other rain forest land is converted to farms that grow
170	coffee, soybeans, and palm trees. Oil from those palm trees can be used to
184	make biofuels. Companies build roads through the rain forests to transport
195	goods to and from the farms. These businesses often play necessary roles
207	in their countries. Without them, their countries' economies would suffer.
217	Rain Forest Loss Can Be Controlled
223	The loss of rain forest trees does threaten wildlife habitats and the
235	quality of the soil. But a complete halt to rain forest cutting would create
249	other serious problems. A more sensible goal is to manage the use of rain
263	forest land so that the negative outcomes are limited.

Name _____

The World Needs Rain Forests

People must preserve the rain forests for the sake of the environment.

Each day, thousands of acres of rain forest are destroyed in the name of progress. Cutting down the rain forest benefits some economies, but it does long-term damage to the planet.

Rain Forests and Biodiversity

Most of Earth's plant and animal species reside in forests. As trees are cut down, these species lose their habitats. Some species cannot survive that habitat loss and become extinct. Species loss decreases Earth's biodiversity, or variety of life. Science has shown that the survival of life depends on biodiversity.

Earth's Water Cycle and Rain Forests

The rain forests play a key part in the water cycle. Rain forest plants release water vapor into the atmosphere. That water vapor turns into rain. As the rain forests disappear, less water vapor is released. This loss can change global rainfall patterns.

Rain Forests Affect the Air We Breathe

Rain forest loss affects the climate in other ways too. The trees in a rain forest help us breathe by releasing oxygen into the atmosphere. They also clean the air by absorbing greenhouse gases. Greenhouse gases feed global warming. Destroying rain forests increases global warming by adding greenhouse gases to the atmosphere.

Rain forests are ecosystems rich in plants and animals. Rain forests are also important economically to the countries they belong to.

Thinking Globally

Nations must look beyond local needs and adopt a global perspective. We need to preserve the rain forests for the benefit of all.

Name _____

A. Reread the passages and answer the questions.

1. What is the first author's point of view about rain forests?

_____

_____

2. What facts from the text support this point of view?

_____

_____

_____

3. What is the second author's point of view about rain forests?

_____

_____

4. What facts from the text support this point of view?

_____

_____

_____

B. Work with a partner. Read the passage aloud. Pay attention to expression and phrasing. Stop after one minute. Fill out the chart.

	Words Read	–	Number of Errors	=	Words Correct Score
First Read		–		=	
Second Read		–		=	

Name _____

Expand Our Urban Forests

Trees play a very important role in the landscape of cities. Noise levels and summer temperatures are higher in cities than in outlying areas. Trees absorb noise and heat and keep cities quieter and cooler. Planting trees helps keep the air clean and save energy. Trees soak up pollutants from the air and give off oxygen. Being around green, wooded areas helps keep people healthy. All cities should plant more trees and expand their forests.

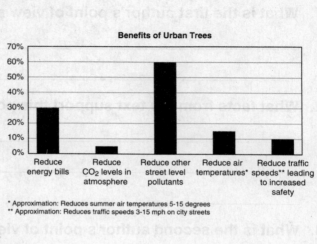

Benefits of Urban Trees

* Approximation: Reduces summer air temperatures 5-15 degrees
** Approximation: Reduces traffic speeds 3-15 mph on city streets

Answer the questions about the text.

1. **What genre of text is this? How do you know?**

_____

_____

2. **What opinion does the author express in the text?**

_____

_____

3. **What text feature does this text include?**

_____

_____

4. **How does the text feature help you better understand the author's viewpoint?**

_____

_____

_____

Name _____

Latin root	Meaning	Examples
vivere	to live	sur<u>viv</u>al, sur<u>viv</u>e
cultura	cultivation	agri<u>cult</u>ure
merc/merx	merchandise	com<u>merc</u>e, com<u>merc</u>ial
portare	to carry	trans<u>port</u>
sedere	to sit	re<u>side</u>
sorbere	to suck in/suck up	ab<u>sorb</u>, ab<u>sorb</u>ing
specere	to look at	per<u>spec</u>tive

Read each passage below. Use the root words in the box and sentence clues to help you figure out the meaning of each word in bold. Write the word's meaning on the line. Then write your own sentence that uses the word in the same way.

1. In most cases, when part of a rain forest is cut down, subsistence **agriculture** takes its place. Subsistence agriculture is farming or ranching that produces only enough for a family to meet its everyday needs.

   _____

   _____

2. The families need these farms or ranches in order to **survive**.

   _____

   _____

3. **Commercial** activities also play a role in the use of rain forest land. Lumber from rain forest trees is used to make furniture, flooring, and paper. Many countries buy beef that comes from cattle ranches on former rain forest land. Other rain forest land is converted to farms that grow coffee, soybeans, and palm trees. Oil from those palm trees can be used to make biofuels.

   _____

   _____

Name _____

Add the suffix *-ion* to the verb in parentheses to complete each sentence. Remember that when a base word ends in the letter e, the e is dropped before the suffix *-ion* is added.

1. The class held a lively **(discuss)** _____ about water conservation.

2. He only needs to make one **(correct)** _____ to complete his work.

3. We purchased a new **(decorate)** _____ that will hang on the bedroom wall.

4. The wind changed **(direct)** _____ before it started to rain.

5. It is smart to study the candidates and the issues before voting in an **(elect)** _____.

6. Our family trip to the national park made a lasting **(impress)** _____.

7. Try to maintain your **(concentrate)** _____ when taking a test.

8. If everyone talks at the same time, it will lead to **(confuse)** _____.

9. In my **(estimate)** _____, that is not a valuable painting.

10. After hiking all day, the campers were overcome with **(exhaust)** _____.

Name _____

Evidence is details and examples from a text that support a writer's ideas. The student who wrote the paragraph below cited evidence to show how an author used reasons and evidence to support his or her position on a topic.

Topic sentence ⟶   In "The World Needs Rain Forests," the author uses reasons and evidence to support the position that people should preserve rain forests. The author's reasons are that

Evidence ⟶ cutting down rain forests will affect the survival of life, the water cycle, and the air we breathe. The author includes facts as evidence. When trees in the rain forest are cut down, some species become extinct and less water vapor and oxygen is released into the atmosphere. All of these reasons and

Concluding statement ⟶ evidence support the author's position that people should preserve rainforests.

Write a paragraph about the text you have chosen. Cite evidence from the text to show how the author used reasons and evidence to support his or her position.

Write a topic sentence: _____

_____

Cite evidence from the text: _____

_____

_____

_____

_____

End with a concluding statement: _____

_____

Name _____

A. Read the draft model. Use the questions that follow the draft to help you think about how you can write a strong conclusion.

Draft Model

So that's why I think volunteering is important. Volunteering is a good thing to do. Learning new skills is good too, but try volunteering. You'll like it.

---

1. What is the most important point of the text?

2. What persuasive language might you use?

3. How can you restate the main idea in a way that persuades the reader to take action?

4. What final important or interesting thought can you present to the reader?

B. Now revise the draft by rewriting sentences to restate the main idea and make the conclusion stronger.

_____

_____

_____

_____

_____

_____

_____

_____

_____

_____

_____

Name _____

| intercept | bulletin | recruits | operations |
| survival | enlisted | diversity | contributions |

Finish each sentence using the vocabulary word provided.

1. **(recruits)** On her first day in the army, my sister _____

_____ .

2. **(contributions)** The food bank will use the _____

_____ .

3. **(intercept)** During the game, he tried _____

_____ .

4. **(operations)** The construction company _____

_____ .

5. **(diversity)** The United States is a nation _____

_____ .

6. **(survival)** A constant supply of food and water _____

_____ .

7. **(bulletin)** I decided not to walk to school because _____

_____ .

8. **(enlisted)** It has been over a year since _____

_____ .

Name _____

Read the selection. Complete the theme graphic organizer.

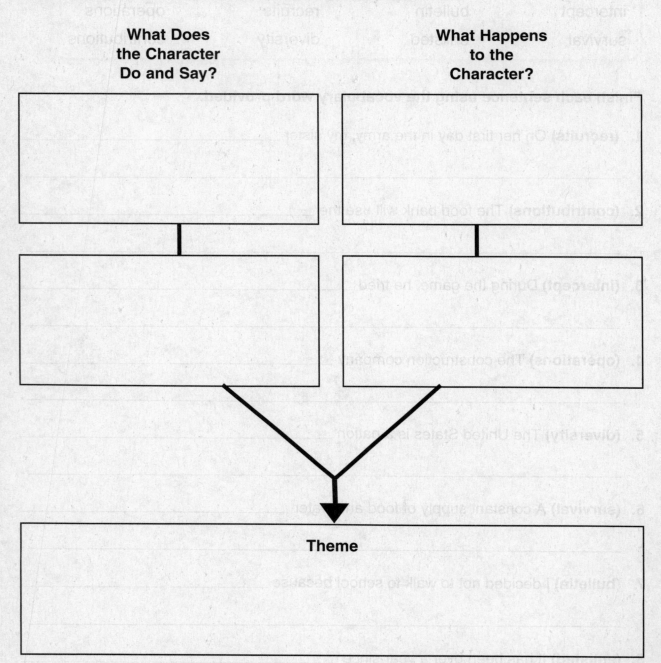

What Does the Character Do and Say?	What Happens to the Character?

Theme

Name _____

Read the passage. Use the summarizing strategy to help you understand what you are reading.

Books for Victory

12	As Carlos shivered on the snowy porch, he noticed a drooping banner in the front window. "Happy New Year 1943!" it said. "Huh, they
24	could've taken that down by now," he thought as he pressed the doorbell
37	once more. "Hurry up," he muttered. "I'm turning blue out here." As he
50	waited for his neighbor to answer the door, Carlos blew on his hands to
64	warm them. Glancing at his wagon piled with books, he thought back to
77	last year and the reason he was out here again collecting for the Victory
91	Book Campaign.
93	His brother Tomás had been in the army and stationed at a military
106	camp across the country. Carlos had missed Tomás and looked forward
117	to his letters. Carlos knew one of those letters by heart. "There's nothing
130	new to tell you," Tomás had written. "We still train and drill every day.
144	When we're not training and drilling there's not much to do. I wish I had
159	something good to read."
163	Carlos had felt bad for Tomás. He wondered how he could help him.
176	The next day, in morning assembly, Principal Ramírez told the students
187	about the Victory Book Campaign. All over Oregon and the rest of the
200	country, people were collecting books to send to soldiers, sailors, and
211	others fighting in the war.
216	Principal Ramírez added that the campaign needed volunteers. As soon
226	as he said that, hands shot up all over the auditorium.
237	Carlos had promised himself he would collect as many books as
248	he possibly could and during the following month he took his wagon
260	throughout the neighborhood. At each house he explained the campaign
270	and asked people to donate books. In its first year, the campaign had lasted
284	from January to November. It had been an outstanding success. By the
296	time it was over, people across the country had donated more than eleven
309	million books.

Name _____

As Mrs. Wright opened the door, Carlos was pulled out of the past and back to the present. Only a few seconds had passed, even though he'd been thinking of a period lasting several months.

"I know just why you're here," Mrs. Wright smiled. "I looked all over the house and I have quite a large stack of books. What kind of books are you looking for this year?"

"We'd like fiction," Carlos answered. "Adventure stories, westerns, mysteries, and detective stories would be good. We also want nonfiction. But I hear that those books should be published after 1935, so they'll be up-to-date."

Carlos had promised himself he would collect as many books as he could.

Mrs. Wright pointed to a tall stack of books by the door. "Good. I think these will all be suitable then," she said. "You know, I'm reading some new novels right now. When will you be by again?"

"I'll be back in a few weeks," Carlos replied as he gathered up the stack of books. "We'll be collecting for a couple more months."

"That's great," Mrs. Wright nodded. "My daughter Grace will be home from college next weekend. I'll ask her to go through her books and see what she'd like to donate."

As he walked to his wagon, Carlos called back, "That's terrific, Mrs. Wright! One of our slogans is *Give More Books, Give Good Books*. I'm sure Grace's books will be good ones, too. Thanks so much for these!"

Carlos and Mrs. Wright waved at each other and he set off for his next stop: the library. There, volunteers would sort through what Carlos and others had brought in. Then large collection centers would ship the books to people in military camps and overseas.

He was still chilled, but Carlos felt proud. He was too young to join the army, like Tomás. He couldn't work in a defense factory, like his parents. But, by collecting books, he and his classmates were making a contribution. Best of all, they were helping his brother Tomás and others fighting for their country.

Name _____

A. Reread the passage and answer the questions.

1. How does Carlos feel when he hears about the Victory Book Campaign?

_____

_____

2. Why does he feel that way?

_____

_____

3. What does Carlos learn from his experience? What might be the theme, or message, of this story?

_____

_____

B. Work with a partner. Read the passage aloud. Pay attention to expression and phrasing. Stop after one minute. Fill out the chart.

	Words Read	–	Number of Errors	=	Words Correct Score
First Read		–		=	
Second Read		–		=	

Name _____

The Scrap Drive

Alice watched the young girl drop the bottle into the recycle bin. She remembered how she had started recycling when she was the girl's age. During World War II, everything was rationed, and people needed to recycle. She recalled how schools in her city had a Scrap Drive contest every month and collected paper, metal, rubber, and fabric. One day she had asked her father, "Dad, how can I help my school win the contest?"

"That old, bald tire in the garage might help," Dad had said. "A rubber tire can be reused to make 20 pairs of boots."

Alice and her dad had found the tire and started to roll it to the collection center at the bottom of the hill. The tire slipped from Dad's grasp and rolled downhill. "Stop that tire!" Dad had shouted. They raced after the tire, but it had crashed into the collection center building. Alice smiled to herself and remembered how proud she had felt when her school had won the contest that month.

Answer the questions about the text.

1. **How do you know this text is historical fiction?**

   _____

   _____

   _____

2. **A flashback is a scene from the past that interrupts a story. What sentence tells that a flashback is coming?**

   _____

   _____

3. **What two time clues signal that this takes place in the past?**

   _____

   _____

Name _____

Read the sentences below and circle the correct word to complete each one. Underline the context clues that help you figure out which word to use. Then use that word in a new sentence.

1. This morning the wind _____ so hard that I nearly fell over.   **blew**   **blue**

_____

_____

2. I thought I _____ all the answers to her questions.   **knew**   **new**

_____

_____

3. I didn't recognize you when we _____ on the street.   **passed**   **past**

_____

_____

4. Call your dog to come _____ now.   **hear**   **here**

_____

_____

5. He seems like a nice person and a good friend, _____.   **to**   **too**

_____

_____

Name _____

A. **Add the word parts to create a word with a Greek root. Write the word on the line. Then circle the word below that has the same Greek root.**

1. tele + vision = _____

    automated   telegram   asteroid

2. auto + mobile = _____

    disaster   automatic   microwave

3. photo + genic = _____

    philosophy   telephoto   program

4. homo + phone = _____

    phonics   mechanic   psychic

5. para + graph = _____

    videophone   invite   graphic

B. **Read each sentence. Replace the underlined words with one of the words from the word box below and rewrite the sentence.**

> mechanical   phonics   autograph   astronomer   photograph

6. The <u>scientist who studies stars and planets</u> was able to see Mars.

    _____

7. My uncle is studying how to take a <u>picture</u> with his new camera.

    _____

8. They were able to get the <u>handwritten name</u> of the famous actress.

    _____

9. I understand <u>the science of sounds</u>, so I can read almost any word.

    _____

10. People who are <u>able to fix machines</u> will always be able to find a job.

    _____

Name _____

Evidence is details and examples from a text that support a writer's ideas. The student who wrote the paragraph below cited evidence to show how the author's descriptions of a character's feelings help to convey the theme.

Topic sentence ⟶   In "Books for Victory," the author's descriptions of Carlos's feelings help to convey the theme that all of us can contribute to a cause. The author shows that Carlos had felt bad that his brother didn't have good books to read in the army. He started collecting books to send to the military and got others involved. After Carlos collects books, he feels proud to help his brother and others. By showing that Carlos feels proud after he collects books, the author conveys the message that everyone can contribute to a cause.

Evidence ⟶

Concluding statement ⟶

Write a paragraph about a text you have chosen. Cite evidence from the text to show how the author's descriptions of a character's feelings help to convey the theme.

Write a topic sentence: _____

_____

Cite evidence from the text: _____

_____

_____

_____

_____

End with a concluding statement: _____

_____

Name _____

A. Read the draft model. Use the questions that follow the draft to help you think about the order, or sequence, of events.

Draft Model

Last week, we held a paper drive. We took the paper to the recycling center. But first we set out bins for magazines and newspapers. We had also advertised.

---

1. Which sentences could be reordered?

2. What sequence word or phrase could be changed in the third sentence?

3. What sequence word or phrase could show when the advertisement was placed?

B. Now revise the draft by adding sequence words to help readers understand more about the sequence of events.

_____

_____

_____

_____

_____

_____

_____

_____

_____

_____

_____

_____

_____

Name _____

> taunting   ally   abruptly   confident
>
> collided   protective   conflict   intervene

Finish each sentence using the vocabulary word provided.

1. **(taunting)** After the victory, the team showed respect by _____

   _____.

2. **(ally)** In order to get my message across, _____

   _____.

3. **(abruptly)** When the fire alarm went off, _____

   _____.

4. **(confident)** At first he was nervous about speaking in class, _____

   _____.

5. **(collided)** We looked outside when we heard the loud crash and _____

   _____.

6. **(protective)** She wanted to walk to the movie alone, but her parents _____

   _____.

7. **(conflict)** We didn't expect the minor disagreement _____

   _____.

8. **(intervene)** The class couldn't agree on a destination for the field trip, _____

   _____.

Name _____

Read the selection. Complete the theme graphic organizer.

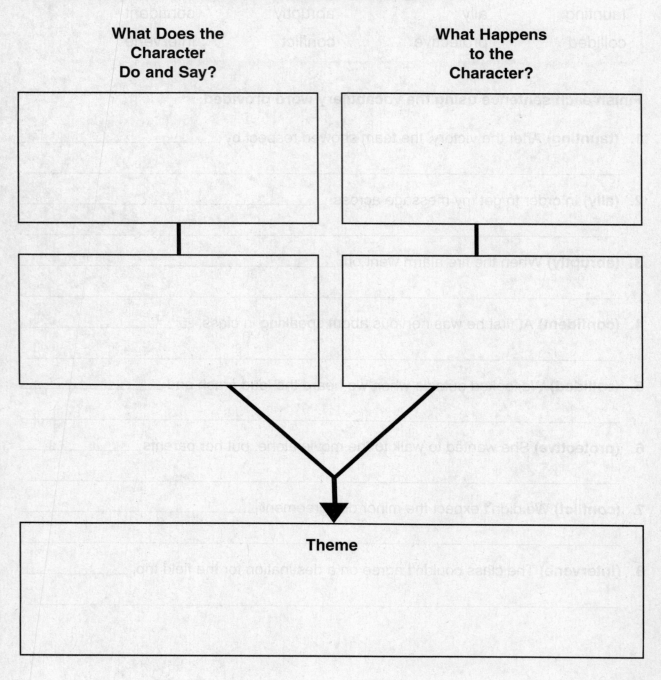

Name _____

Read the passage. Use the summarizing strategy to help you understand what you are reading.

The Battle of the Bedroom

	My older sister, Marta, glares at me from across the room. Her dark
13	brown eyes blaze with anger; she's ready to burst. I almost say something
26	to set her off, but Dad said if he heard any more noise from our room that
43	we would both be grounded.
48	Sure, we fight like all sisters do, but the battle lines were redrawn when
62	we moved into our new house a week ago. In our old house, we each
77	had our own bedroom. Now we have to share, and it has led to an all-out
93	war. We still haven't unpacked a thing because we can't agree on how to
107	decorate the room. Right now, we're stuck with cardboard boxes.
117	Marta wants dark walls, gray curtains, and posters of her favorite bands.
129	I want a mural of ocean creatures against bright blue walls. Our family
142	took a trip to the Gulf of Mexico last year, and I fell in love with the
159	sparkling blue water. I think it would be fun to have a reminder of that.
174	Marta despises my idea, and I sure don't like hers, so now we're stuck in
189	a stalemate.
191	Dad pops his head into the room. "Lucia, Marta, can we see you in the
206	living room, please?" He and Mom are sitting on the couch. Marta and I
220	sit in chairs across from them.
226	Dad starts by telling us how disappointed he is, especially about
237	the disrespect we've shown them and each other. I squirm in my seat,
250	embarrassed that we've been acting so childish.
257	Mom cuts to the chase and says, "It's a mystery to us how two bright
272	and reasonable girls can be so inflexible." She hands us each a spiral
285	notebook and a ballpoint pen. "You both have good ideas. So we're giving
298	you one hour to come up with a plan..." she looks back and forth between
313	us, "for the other person's idea. Lucia, you'll tell us why Marta's idea is
327	the best, and vice versa."

Name _____

"That isn't fair," Marta screeches, her shrill voice rising another octave. "Lucia's idea is childish and awful!"

I leap to defend myself but quickly choke back my words. Our parents' faces are bleak.

We both storm into our bedroom and resume our positions; she's on her bed, and I'm across the room on mine. We lock eyes for a few moments before she sighs and slumps against the wall. "So why do you want to do this ocean thing?" she asks in a monotone voice, acting like she doesn't care.

Sharing a bedroom isn't getting off to a good start, especially since we can't agree on how to decorate it.

"Remember our vacation last year?" I cross my arms and glare at her. "It was so much fun, and we didn't fight all week, not even when it rained all day and we stayed in the hotel room. It would be nice to have a reminder of that." I look up, surprised to see the tension draining from her face.

"I didn't know that it meant so much to you," she murmurs, sounding almost apologetic. She thinks for a moment, then explains, "This is our only chance, Lucia. We get to decorate once, and you might not want to see starfish every day for the next five years. If we choose a simpler design, we can enjoy it longer."

I hadn't considered that before. "The walls don't have to be blue," I say quietly, uncrossing my arms. "I like other colors, too."

"A darker blue could be nice, maybe with white trim?" Marta gives me a shy smile. She mentions that Mom took a lot of photos during that trip, most of them of the ocean. "Maybe we could use those for artwork instead of my old posters," she offers.

I beam at her. "I would like that a lot."

Marta scrambles onto my bed and together we brainstorm ideas for our shared living space. I have a sneaking suspicion that this was Mom and Dad's plan all along, but Marta and I are having such a good time that I'll let it slide...this time.

Name _____

A. Reread the passage and answer the questions.

1. What problem does sharing a bedroom create for Marta and Lucia?

_____

_____

2. Why do the girls' parents give them each a notebook and a pen?

_____

_____

3. What happens when the sisters discuss their ideas with each other?

_____

_____

_____

4. What is the theme of the passage?

_____

_____

B. Work with a partner. Read the passage aloud. Pay attention to intonation. Stop after one minute. Fill out the chart.

	Words Read	–	Number of Errors	=	Words Correct Score
First Read		–		=	
Second Read		–		=	

Name _____

Paying it Forward

Andy frowned at his cast-enclosed leg. He'd broken his tibia and fibula, and cracked his patella—three important leg bones—the doctor had said.

Suddenly, his mom walked in. His classmate Peter followed her, grasping something secretively in his hand.

Oh, great! Andy thought. *Peter's come to be mean to me, like always.*

"Just go home!" he snapped.

"Chill out," Peter replied. "I broke an arm last summer, and a friend made it better for me. I've come to do the same for you." He held out a video game. "I just picked up a copy of a great new video game," Peter said. "Want to play?"

Answer the questions about the text.

1. Name a detail that lets you know this text is realistic fiction. How does it do that?

   _____

   _____

2. Write an example of a descriptive detail from the text. How does the detail add to the text's setting, characters, or events?

   _____

   _____

3. How does the author use pacing in this text? How does the pacing help make the text seem realistic?

   _____

   _____

Name _____

Read each passage. Then, on the lines below the passage, give the denotation, or definition, and connotation of the words in bold. Identify the connotation as positive, negative, or neutral.

1. My older sister, Marta, glares at me from across the room. Her dark brown eyes **blaze** with anger; she's ready to burst.

   _____

2. Sure, we fight like all sisters do, but the **battle lines** were redrawn when we moved into our new house a week ago.

   _____

3. Marta **despises** my idea, and I sure don't like hers, so now we're stuck in a stalemate.

   _____

4. "That isn't fair," Marta **screeches**, her shrill voice rising another octave. "Lucia's idea is childish and awful!"

   _____

5. I leap to defend myself but quickly **choke** back my words. Our parents' faces are bleak.

   _____

Name _____

Latin Roots and Their Meanings

tract: to pull	**miss/mitt:** to send
port: to carry	**aud:** to hear
spect: to look at	**vis:** to see

Complete each sentence with a word from the word box below. A definition of each missing word is given in parentheses ( ).

audible	tractor	portable	import	spectator
distract	vision	inaudible	dismiss	visible

1. The tall mountains were _____ from our balcony. (able to be seen)

2. The farmer used his _____ to tow the wagon. (vehicle that is used to pull farm equipment)

3. The new line of luggage was designed to be _____. (easy to carry)

4. It was so loud outside that the music was nearly _____. (unable to be heard)

5. The principal decided to _____ the students earlier than usual. (send away)

6. Every _____ in the stadium cheered when the winning touchdown was scored. (person who goes to look at an event)

Name _____

Evidence is details and examples from a text that support a writer's opinions. The student who wrote the paragraph below cited evidence to show how well the author developed realistic characters and events.

Topic sentence →   I think the author of "The Battle of the Bedroom" does a good job of making the characters and events seem realistic.

Evidence →   Marta and Lucia are sisters. They can't agree on how to decorate their shared room. Real sisters have problems like this. They don't always want the same things. At the end of the story, Marta and Lucia talk about their ideas and come to a compromise. This is what real sisters do to work out

Concluding statement →   problems. I think the author showed how the characters solve their problem in a realistic way.

Write a paragraph about a realistic fiction story. Cite evidence from the text to show how well the author developed realistic characters and events.

Write a topic sentence: _____
_____

Cite evidence from the text: _____
_____
_____
_____
_____

End with a concluding statement: _____
_____

Name _____

A. Read the draft model. Use the questions that follow the draft to help you think about what time-order words you can add.

Draft Model

Maria and I could not agree on a science project. I wanted to grow crystals. Maria wanted to make a volcano. We chose a project we both liked—making a robot.

---

1. What time-order words could show when the event in the first sentence takes place?

2. How are the ideas in the second and third sentences related? What words could show this?

3. What time-order word could you use to state when the last sentence happened?

B. Now revise the draft by choosing words that tell the time order of the events in the paragraph.

_____

_____

_____

_____

_____

_____

_____

_____

Name _____

| adaptation | cache | forage | hibernate |
| agile | dormant | frigid | insulates |

Use each pair of vocabulary words in a single sentence.

1. frigid, insulates

_____

_____

2. dormant, hibernate

_____

_____

3. adaptation, cache

_____

_____

4. agile, forage

_____

_____

Name _____

Read the selection. Complete the cause and effect graphic organizer.

Cause	➡	Effect
	➡	
	➡	
	➡	
	➡	

Name _____

Read the passage. Use the ask and answer questions strategy to help you understand what you read.

Life in the Desert

13	What do you think of when you hear the word *desert*? You probably
27	picture a place that is hot and dry. Although there are some desert areas
42	that are cold, most deserts are as you imagine them. They are dry and hot.
	A desert is an area that gets less than ten inches of rain each year. Many
58	types of animals live in these harsh climates. Survival for desert animals
70	depends on their ability to adapt, or change.

Structural Adaptation

80	One kind of adaptation is structural. This means the animal's body has
92	changed so that it can survive in the climate. The gundi is an example of
107	this adaptation. A gundi is a small animal that looks a lot like a guinea
122	pig. Gundis live in the deserts of Africa. The desert has very little drinking
136	water, but gundis get all the moisture they need from their diet of plants.
150	Gundis' fur helps them stay cool during the day and warm at night.

Behavioral Adaptation

165	Another type of adaptation is behavioral. Desert animals act in ways
176	that help them survive. Since it is so hot during the day, many animals are
191	nocturnal. They rest under rocks or in other cool places during the day and
205	come out at night to hunt for food.

Thriving in the Desert

217	Most desert animals adapt in a combination of ways. Dromedary
227	camels live in the deserts of Africa and the Arabian Peninsula. They raise
240	their body temperature to reduce loss of water, and they can live for days
254	without eating or drinking. Dromedaries have a hump on their backs that
266	is made up of fat. They use the fat for energy when food is scarce. These
282	animals sweat very little, which saves water. When they do drink, they can
295	take in as many as thirty gallons of water in a little over ten minutes!

Name _____

The fennec fox is a tiny fox that weighs only about three pounds as an adult. Like dromedaries, fennec foxes live in the African and Arabian deserts. Their sand-colored fur makes it difficult for their enemies to see them. The light color also keeps them cool during the day. Fennec foxes even have fur on the bottoms of their feet. This makes it easier to walk on the hot desert sand. Their bodies lose water very slowly, so they can go for days without drinking. Fennec foxes rest in burrows during the day. At night they hunt for eggs, insects, and other small animals.

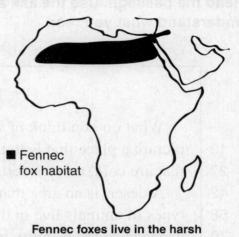

■ Fennec fox habitat

Fennec foxes live in the harsh desert climates of Africa and the Arabian Peninsula.

The deserts of the southwestern United States and northern Mexico are home to a large lizard called a Gila monster. Gila monsters store fat in their abdomens and tails, which lets them live for months without eating. They come out only at night during the summer. In winter the lizards hibernate. During this period of inactivity, they use very little food and energy.

Many different types of snakes live in the desert. Because they are cold-blooded, snakes' body temperatures change with that of their surroundings. To avoid becoming too hot, they find shelter under bushes or rocks. Some rattlesnakes, for example, are nocturnal and bury themselves in the sand during the day. In the hottest part of the year, many snakes rest for a long period. This is similar to the winter hibernation of some other animals.

Meerkats are members of the mongoose family that live in Africa. They hunt early in the day to avoid the heat. They live in mobs, or groups, of as many as thirty members. The mob helps keep its members safe. Predators, such as eagles or jackals, are often frightened away by a meerkat mob.

Even though deserts are one of Earth's harshest environments, the animals that live in them have bodies that are adapted for extreme conditions. These adaptations help the animals avoid heat, store food and water, and protect themselves from enemies.

Name _____

A. Reread the passage and answer the questions.

1. **What causes many desert animals to adapt their behavior so that they sleep during the day instead of at night?**

   _____

   _____

2. **What evidence in the fifth paragraph shows the structural effects of a desert climate on an animal's body?**

   _____

   _____

   _____

3. **What are three ways the fennec fox has adapted to its harsh desert climate?**

   _____

   _____

   _____

   _____

B. Work with a partner. Read the passage aloud. Pay attention to rate and accuracy. Stop after one minute. Fill out the chart.

	Words Read	–	Number of Errors	=	Words Correct Score
First Read		–		=	
Second Read		–		=	

Name _____

Desert Plant Adaptations

Plants adapt to living in the Mojave Desert in many ways. One way plants survive is by conserving water. They have spines or thorns that direct air flow and reflect hot sunlight. Waxy leaves hold moisture in to reduce water loss. Shallow roots help plants use every bit of rainfall. Other plants have long roots that allow them to get water from deep in the ground. Desert flowers bloom only when it rains. These adaptations enable a wide variety of plants to survive in the desert.

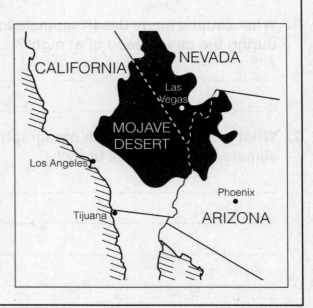

Answer the questions about the text.

1. How do you know this is expository text?

   _____

   _____

2. What is the heading? Is it a strong heading for this text? Why or why not?

   _____

   _____

3. What other text feature does this text include? What information does it give you?

   _____

   _____

Name _____

Read each passage. Underline the context clues that help you figure out the meaning of each word in bold. Then, in your own words, write the definition of the word.

1. One kind of adaptation is **structural**. This means the animal's body has changed so that it can survive in the climate.

   _____

2. Another type of adaptation is **behavioral**. Desert animals act in ways that help them survive.

   _____

3. Since it is so hot during the day, many animals are **nocturnal**. They rest under rocks or in other cool places during the day and come out at night to hunt for food.

   _____

4. Gila monsters come out only at night during the summer. In winter the lizards **hibernate**. During this period of inactivity, they use very little food and energy.

   _____

5. Many different types of snakes live in the desert. Because they are **cold-blooded**, snakes' body temperatures change with that of their surroundings.

   _____

   _____

6. Meerkats are members of the mongoose family that live in Africa. They hunt early in the day to avoid the heat. They live in **mobs**, or groups, of as many as thirty members. The mob helps keep its members safe.

   _____

Name _____

**Read each sentence below. Circle the word that has origins in mythology.
Then write the meaning of the word on the line. You may use a dictionary.**

> **Janus:** Roman god of beginnings
>
> **Atlas:** Greek giant who supported the world on his shoulders
>
> **Luna:** Roman goddess of the moon
>
> **Clotho:** Greek goddess who spins the thread of human life
>
> **Oceanus:** Greek god of the stream of water encircling the world
>
> **Olympus:** mountain in Greece known as home of the gods
>
> **Furies:** Greek goddesses of law and punishment
>
> **Fortuna:** Roman goddess of luck

1. The ocean is home to a wide variety of plants and animals.

   _____

2. They used an atlas to plan their trip around the world.

   _____

3. Some people start a new hobby or exercise routine in January.

   _____

4. Many people watched the first lunar landing on television.

   _____

5. The other team was furious when the referee made an incorrect call.

   _____

6. In the winter, people wear several layers of clothes to keep warm.

   _____

7. The summer Olympics in 2008 were held in China.

   _____

8. In many fairy tales the main characters set out to seek their fortune.

   _____

Name _____

> *Evidence* is details and examples from a text that support a writer's ideas. The student who wrote the paragraph below cited evidence to show how well the author used cause-and-effect relationships to explain a topic.

Topic sentence →   I think the author of "Life in the Desert" did a good job of using causes and effect to explain adaptations of desert animals. The author shows the effects of the hot and dry

Evidence →   desert on animals that live there. Dromedary camels raise their body temperature so they don't lose water. Fennec foxes also lose water very slowly so they can go for days without drinking. Snakes find shelter under bushes or rocks to avoid

Concluding statement →   becoming too hot. The author does a good job of explaining how all of these animals can survive in the desert.

Write a paragraph about the text you chose. Give your opinion about how well an author used cause-and-effect relationships to explain a topic. Cite text evidence to support your opinion.

Write a topic sentence: _____

_____

Cite evidence from the text: _____

_____

_____

_____

_____

End with a concluding statement: _____

_____

Name _____

A. Read the draft model. Use the questions that follow the draft to help you think about how you can rewrite sentences to vary the structure and make the writing more interesting to read.

Draft Model

I would rather live in an extremely cold environment. I like cold weather. I can put on a sweater. I can also put on a coat.

---

1. Which sentences can you combine to add interest for the reader?

2. How can you vary the rhythm of the sentences?

3. What other kinds of sentence structures would make the writing more interesting?

B. Now revise the draft by rewriting sentences to vary sentence structure and to make the writing easier and more interesting to read.

_____

_____

_____

_____

_____

_____

_____

_____

_____

_____

_____

Name _____

export   glistening   influence   landscape

native   plantations   restore   urged

Write a complete sentence to answer each question below. In your answer, use the vocabulary word in bold.

1. Where would be a good place to photograph a **landscape**? _____

_____

2. How would you make a **glistening** decoration? _____

_____

3. What might **influence** you to buy something? _____

_____

4. Where are fruit **plantations** likely to be located? _____

_____

5. What is something that is found in your **native** country? _____

_____

6. When has someone **urged** you to do something? _____

_____

7. How could someone **restore** an old desk? _____

_____

8. Why might a company decide to **export** a particular product? _____

_____

Name _____

Read the selection. Complete the problem and solution graphic organizer.

Problem	Solution

Name _____

Read the passage. Use the ask and answer questions strategy to guide your reading.

The Father of Earth Day

12	Imagine a world where black clouds of pollution blanketed the sky and
26	rivers ran orange from toxic waste. What would the world be like if the
40	soil was too poisoned to grow food and bald eagles had been hunted to
53	extinction? That world might exist today, if not for the actions of Senator
	Gaylord Nelson.

| 55 | **A Commitment to Conservation** |

59	Gaylord Nelson developed an affection for nature growing up in the
70	woods of northern Wisconsin. As an adult, he brought his love of the
83	land to his political career. When he became governor of Wisconsin in
95	1959, he worked hard to protect and care for his state's natural resources.
108	His Outdoor Recreation Acquisition Program preserved thousands of
116	acres of unspoiled land. The program bought private lands and turned
127	them into wildlife habitats and public parks. Nelson also created a
138	Youth Conservation Corps. The Corps taught young people about the
148	environment while giving them jobs cleaning and caring for the state's
159	natural areas.
161	In 1962 Nelson was elected to the U.S. Senate. He hoped to do
174	for the country what he had done for the state of Wisconsin: protect
187	the environment. He found that few of his fellow senators shared his
199	concerns. Nelson hoped President John F. Kennedy could generate support
209	for environmental issues. In 1963 the senator helped plan a national
220	conservation tour for the president, but the tour did not create the support
233	for environmental issues that Nelson hoped it would.

Name _____

Taking It to the People

Senator Nelson decided to find another way to show Congress that it was important to care for the environment. In 1969, after visiting the site of an oil spill, he read about college students protesting against the Vietnam War. Why not plan a protest against pollution?

At the time, pollution was a big problem. There were no laws about clean air or clean water. Nelson wanted Congress to pass such laws, but he needed to show that people supported the legislation. He hoped a nationwide protest would do that.

Earth Day's message helped make changes that better protect our environment.

Nelson called for pro-environment demonstrations around the country. The protests were held on April 22, 1970, the day Nelson called Earth Day. About 20 million people across the country took part.

Congress heard the message. It created the Environmental Protection Agency. During the next few years, Congress passed some of the country's most important environmental legislation. These laws included the Clean Water Act, the Clean Air Act, and the Endangered Species Act.

Gaylord Nelson left the Senate and politics in 1981, but he did not stop his conservation work. He took a job with the Wilderness Society, an organization that works to protect public wild lands. In 1995, President Bill Clinton gave Nelson the Presidential Medal of Honor for his environmental work.

Nelson's Legacy

Gaylord Nelson died in 2005, but Earth Day lived on. Every year since 1970, people around the world have gathered on April 22 to celebrate the environment. The message of the demonstrations, however, has changed over the years. Instead of calling for political action, Earth Day protests now focus on what private individuals can do to help the environment. As Gaylord Nelson showed, one person can do quite a lot.

Name _____

A. Reread the passage and answer the questions.

1. **What problem did Gaylord Nelson encounter in the U.S. Senate when he tried to get support for environmental issues?**

_____

_____

_____

2. **What gave Senator Nelson an idea for a solution?**

_____

_____

_____

3. **In what way did Senator Nelson's call for demonstrations on Earth Day help the environment?**

_____

_____

_____

_____

B. Work with a partner. Read the passage aloud. Pay attention to expression and phrasing. Stop after one minute. Fill out the chart.

	Words Read	–	Number of Errors	=	Words Correct Score
First Read		–		=	
Second Read		–		=	

Name _____

Conserving the Wild

Dr. Edgar Wayburn spent most of his days saving lives as a physician. However, he spent his spare time saving wilderness areas and creating national parks. As president of the Sierra Club for many years, he urged politicians to protect wild landscapes. His greatest achievement was the Alaska National Interests Land Conservation Act, or ANILCA. In 1999, Dr. Wayburn received the Presidential Medal of Freedom. The award honored his remarkable influence on environmentalism. Dr. Wayburn died in 2010 at the age of 103.

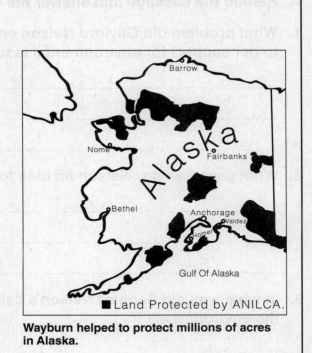

■ Land Protected by ANILCA.

Wayburn helped to protect millions of acres in Alaska.

Answer the questions about the text.

1. **What genre of text is this? How do you know?**

   _____

   _____

2. **What aspect or part of Dr. Wayburn's life is featured in this text?**

   _____

   _____

3. **How does the text feature relate to the text?**

   _____

   _____

4. **How does the heading relate to both the text and the text feature?**

   _____

   _____

Name _____

Read each passage and underline the word that is either a synonym or an antonym for the word in bold. Use the synonym or antonym to write a definition of the word in bold.

1. Gaylord Nelson developed an **affection** for nature growing up in the woods of northern Wisconsin. As an adult, he brought his love of the land to his political career.

   _____

2. When he became governor of Wisconsin in 1959, he worked hard to protect and care for his state's natural resources. His Outdoor Recreation Acquisition Program **preserved** thousands of acres of unspoiled land.

   _____

3. The program purchased **private** lands and converted them into wildlife habitats and public parks.

   _____

4. Nelson hoped President John F. Kennedy could **generate** support for environmental issues. In 1963 the senator helped plan a national conservation tour for the president, but the tour did not produce the amount of support for environmental issues that Nelson hoped it would.

   _____

5. Nelson wanted Congress to pass such laws, but he needed to show that people supported the **legislation**.

   _____

6. Nelson called for pro-environment **demonstrations** around the country. The protests were held on April 22, 1970, the day Nelson called Earth Day.

   _____

Name _____

unison	triplet	unicorn	tripod
biweekly	bicycle	tricycle	unicycle
triangle	bisect	trio	uniform
centimeter	century	binoculars	universe

Read each definition below. Use clues in the definition, such as numbers and root words, to write the word from the box that matches the definition.

1. a shape with three angles _____

2. one hundredth of a meter _____

3. to separate into two sections _____

4. a cycle with three wheels _____

5. a mythical animal with one horn _____

6. a piece of clothing for one purpose _____

7. happening every two weeks _____

8. a stand with three legs _____

9. a period of one hundred years _____

10. an optical device with two sets of lenses _____

11. a cycle with only one wheel _____

12. a group of three people _____

Name _____

Evidence is details and examples from a text that support a writer's ideas. The student who wrote the paragraph below cited evidence to compare how two authors present information in biographies.

Topic sentence → The biographies "The Father of Earth Day" and "Words to Save the World" both show how a real person acted to protect the environment. In "The Father of Earth Day," the author describes the problems Gaylord Nelson worked to solve as a governor and senator. The author of "Words to Save the World" first tells about Rachel Carson's early life and her work as a writer. Then the author tells how Rachel worked to solve the problem of pollution. Both biographies tell about a person who protected nature but present information in different ways.

Evidence →

Concluding statement →

Write a paragraph about two biographies. Cite evidence from the texts to compare how the authors present information differently.

Write a topic sentence: _____

_____

Cite evidence from the text: _____

_____

_____

_____

_____

End with a concluding statement: _____

_____

Name _____

A. Read the draft model. Use the questions that follow the draft to help you think about how to better focus on the topic.

Draft Model

Sonia Cruz deserves a good citizen award. She volunteers as a crossing guard for our school. She enjoys hiking and fishing. She also volunteers in the library every Friday. Her favorite book is *The Giver*.

---

1. Which sentence states the topic of this paragraph?

2. Which sentences focus on what it means to be a "good citizen"?

3. Which sentences do not relate to the idea of a "good citizen"?

4. Does the author provide too much information or not enough information about the topic? How could the focus of the writing be strengthened?

B. Now revise the draft by focusing on the topic.

_____

_____

_____

_____

_____

_____

_____

_____

_____

_____

_____

Name _____

| blares | errand | exchange | connection |

Finish each sentence using the vocabulary word provided.

1. **(blares)** He covers his ears _____

   _____.

2. **(errand)** My grandmother _____

   _____.

3. **(exchange)** This sweater is nice, but _____

   _____.

4. **(connection)** The refrigerator did not work because ____

   _____.

Name _____

Read the selection. Complete the point of view graphic organizer.

Details	Point of View

Name _____

Read the poem. Check your understanding as you read by asking yourself how the speaker thinks and feels.

Running

	Feet pound the pavement,
4	Arms pump up and down,
9	Sun's up and smiling,
13	As I jog through the town.
19	Neighbors out raking,
22	Look up, holler, "Hi!"
26	Trees all wave to me,
31	As I dash on by.
36	Wind kicks up its heels,
41	And gives playful chase.
45	Whooshing and whirling,
48	"Come, let's have a race."
53	I round the corner,
57	Delighted to meet,
60	Two other runners,
63	Who sprint down the street.
68	What is it we share?
73	Well, I think I know—
78	All the world's moving,
82	With places to go.
86	An inch or a mile, jet-fast or snail-slow,
94	We share the journey, together we go.

Name _____

A. Reread the poem and answer the questions.

1. Is this poem a lyric or a narrative poem and how do you know?

_____

_____

2. Write two examples of personification from the poem.

_____

_____

3. What point of view is used in the poem? Write a line that shows the point of view.

_____

_____

B. Work with a partner. Read the passage aloud. Pay attention to expression and phrasing. Stop after one minute. Fill out the chart.

	Words Read	–	Number of Errors	=	Words Correct Score
First Read		–		=	
Second Read		–		=	

Name _____

Big Sky

Standing on a small rise in the road
I saw the big sky.
I had not thought about the name
Big Sky Country
Until that moment,
And I was overwhelmed.
I thought I might explode
At the splendor.
The sun rising from the east
Bounced off soaring clouds
In the west
And shot the sky with coral.
I could turn in circles
And see the sky everywhere I looked.
Nothing blocked my view.
No trees. No mountains. No skyscrapers.
Just sky. Big sky.

Answer the questions about the text.

1. **What is the topic of this poem?**

   _____

   _____

2. **How does the speaker in the poem feel? How do you know?**

   _____

   _____

3. **Is this lyric poetry or narrative poetry? How do you know?**

   _____

   _____

Name _____

Assonance is the repetition of the same vowel sound in two or more words.

Consonance is the repetition of a consonant sound in the *middle* or at the *end* of words.

Read the lines of the lyric poem below. Then answer the questions.

> # Running
>
> Feet pound the pavement,
>   Arms pump up and down,
> Sun's up and smiling,
>   As I jog through the town.
>
> Neighbors out raking,
>   Look up, holler, "Hi!"
> Trees all wave to me,
>   As I dash on by.
>
> Wind kicks up its heels,
>   And gives playful chase.
> Whooshing and whirling,
>   "Come, let's have a race."

1. **Find two examples of assonance in the poem. Write them below.**

   _____

2. **Find two examples of consonance in the poem. Write them below.**

   _____

3. **How do the assonance and consonance affect the poem?**

   _____

   _____

Name _____

Read each sentence. Circle the examples of personification. Then explain the author's meaning in your own words. Use context clues to help you understand the figurative language.

1. "Sun's up and smiling, / As I jog through the town."

   _____

   _____

   _____

2. "Trees all wave to me, / As I dash on by."

   _____

   _____

   _____

3. "Wind kicks up its heels, / And gives playful chase"

   _____

   _____

   _____

Name _____

A. Add the suffix in parentheses to the word in bold.

New Word

1. (able) **enjoy** _____

2. (able) **use** _____

3. (ible) **convert** _____

4. (able) **comfort** _____

5. (ible) **force** _____

6. (ible) **sense** _____

B. Add the suffix *-ible* or *-able* to create a new word. Write the new word on the first line. Then write the meaning of the word on the second line.

	New Word	**Meaning**
7. afford	_____	_____
8. respect	_____	_____
9. collapse	_____	_____
10. honor	_____	_____

Name _____

Evidence is details and examples from a text that support a writer's ideas. The student who wrote the paragraph below cited evidence to support his or her opinion about imagery in a poem.

Topic sentence →   I think the poet who wrote "Running" created strong imagery. The words "Feet pound the pavement" and "Arms pump up and down" help me picture how hard the speaker is running. The words "trees all wave to me" and "As I dash on by" help me picture the wind blowing through the trees as the speaker runs quickly. All of these words create a strong image of the speaker running down the street.

Evidence →

Concluding statement →

Write a paragraph about the poem you have chosen. Give your opinion about how well the poet created strong imagery. Cite words in the poem that created a clear picture in your mind.

Write a topic sentence: _____

_____

Cite evidence from the text: _____

_____

_____

_____

_____

End with a concluding statement: _____

_____

Name _____

A. Read the draft model. Use the questions that follow the draft to help you think about what strong adverbs you can add.

Draft Model

One arm stroke following another, I keep pace.
Then buoyed by my team, I move forward and win.

---

1. What strong adverbs can you add to the first line to describe how the speaker keeps pace?

2. What strong adverbs can you add to the second line to describe the way the speaker moves forward and wins?

3. What strong adverbs could show how the speaker is buoyed by the team?

B. Now revise the draft by adding adverbs to help readers form a better picture of what the speaker in the poem is doing. Then add two more lines to the poem.